Bloom's Classic Critical Views

OSCAR WILDE

Bloom's Classic Critical Views

Bloom's Classic Critical Views

OSCAR WILDE

Edited and with an Introduction by
Harold Bloom
Sterling Professor of the Humanities
Yale University

**BLOOM'S
LITERARY CRITICISM**
An imprint of Infobase Publishing

Bloom's Classic Critical Views: Oscar Wilde

Bloom's Literary Criticism
An imprint of Infobase Publishing
132 West 31st Street
New York NY 10001

Library of Congress Cataloging-in-Publication Data
Oscar Wilde / edited and with an introduction by Harold Bloom.
    p. cm.— (Bloom's classic critical views)
    Includes bibliographical references and index.
    ISBN 978-1-60413-140-6 (acid-free paper) 1. Wilde, Oscar, 1854–1900—Criticism and interpretation. I. Bloom, Harold. II. Title. III. Series.

    PR5824.O82 2008
    828'.809—dc22
                                        2008011869

Bloom's Literary Criticism books are available at special discounts when purchased in bulk quantities for businesses, associations, institutions, or sales promotions. Please call our Special Sales Department in New York at (212) 967-8800 or (800) 322-8755.

You can find Bloom's Literary Criticism on the World Wide Web at
http://www.chelseahouse.com

Contributing editor: Paul Fox
Series design by Erika K. Arroyo
Cover design by Takeshi Takahashi
Printed in the United States of America
Bang EJB 10 9 8 7 6 5 4 3 2 1

This book is printed on acid-free paper.

All links and Web addresses were checked and verified to be correct at the time of publication. Because of the dynamic nature of the Web, some addresses and links may have changed since publication and may no longer be valid.

Contents

Series Introduction

Bloom's Classic Critical Views is a new series presenting a selection of the most important older literary criticism on the greatest authors commonly read in high school and college classes today. Unlike the Bloom's Modern Critical Views series, which for more than 20 years has provided the best contemporary criticism on great authors, Bloom's Classic Critical Views attempts to present the authors in the context of their time and to provide criticism that has proved over the years to be the most valuable to readers and writers. Selections range from contemporary reviews in popular magazines, which demonstrate how a work was received in its own era, to profound essays by some of the strongest critics in the British and American tradition, including Henry James, G.K. Chesterton, Matthew Arnold, and many more.

Some of the critical essays and extracts presented here have appeared previously in other titles edited by Harold Bloom, such as the New Moulton's Library of Literary Criticism. Other selections appear here for the first time in any book by this publisher. All were selected under Harold Bloom's guidance.

In addition, each volume in this series contains a series of essays by a contemporary expert, who comments on the most important critical selections, putting them in context and suggesting how they might be used by a student writer to influence his or her own writing. This series is intended above all for students, to help them think more deeply and write more powerfully about great writers and their works.

Introduction by Harold Bloom

The Divine Oscar, as I delight in naming him, was the overt disciple of the Sublime Walter Pater, whose anxiety of influence in regard to John Ruskin resulted in no mentions of Ruskin anywhere in Pater's writings. We remember Wilde for his stage comedies, *The Importance of Being Earnest* in particular, and tend to forget that he was also a strong literary critic. My favorite among his critical ventures is a delightful dialogue, "The Decay of Lying." Here is Vivian, Wilde's surrogate, in a grand epiphany:

> No great artist ever sees things as they really are. If he did, he would cease to be an artist. Take an example from our own day, I know that you are fond of Japanese things. Now, do you really imagine that the Japanese people, as they are presented to us in art, have any existence? If you do, you have never understood Japanese art at all. The Japanese people are the deliberate self-conscious creation of certain individual artists. If you set a picture by Hokusai, or Hokkei, or any of the great native painters, beside a real Japanese gentleman or lady, you will see that there is not the slightest resemblance between them. The actual people who live in Japan are not unlike the general run of English people; that is to say, they are extremely commonplace, and have nothing curious or extraordinary about them. In fact that whole of Japan is a pure invention. There is no such country, there are no such people. One of our most charming painters went recently to the Land of the Chrysanthemum in the foolish hope of seeing the Japanese. All he saw, all he had the chance of painting, were a few lanterns and some fans.

The greatness of this centers in the outrageously funny: "In fact the whole of Japan is a pure invention. There is no such country. There are no such people." Wilde's wisdom leads to a memorable redefinition of the highest criticism:

> That is what the highest criticism really is, the record of one's own soul. It is more fascinating than history, as it is concerned simply with oneself. It is more delightful than philosophy, as its subject is concrete and not abstract, real and not vague. It is the only civilized form of autobiography as it deals not with the events, but with the thoughts of one's life; not with life's physical accidents of death and circumstance, but with the spiritual moods and imaginative passions of the mind.

To call criticism "the only civilized form of autobiography" is beautifully to transform accepted ideas both of criticism and of autobiography. When I want biography of Samuel Johnson, I happily return to Boswell. When I require Johnson on Johnson, I turn to *The Lines of the Poets*, his critical masterwork. For sly parody of Johnson, I cheerfully resort to Lady Augusta Bracknell in Wilde's *The Importance of Being Earnest*. Nonsense literature— Lewis Carroll, Edward Lear, Gilbert and Sullivan—is the genre *Earnest* joins itself to; *Patience* and *Iolanthe* are particularly close by. ·

I am found of quoting what I call "Wilde's Law," splendidly set forth by Algernon in the original, four-act version of *Earnest*:

> My experience of life is that whenever one tells a lie one is corroborated on every side. When one tells the truth one is left in a very lonely and painful position, and no one believes a word one says.

This reverberates strongly in the company of Vivian's declaration in "The Decay of Lying":

> They never rise beyond the level to misrepresentation, and actually condescend to prove, to discuss, to argue. How different from the temper of the true liar, with his frank, fearless statements, his superb irresponsibility, his healthy, natural disdain of proof of any kind! After all, what is a fine lie? Simply that which is its own evidence. If a man is sufficiently unimaginative to produce evidence in support of a lie, he might just as well speak the truth at once.

Oscar profoundly understood that the truth is death, so that the imagination could survive only by creating fictions of the self. His personal tragedy came from being born out of date. In our time, his homoeroticsm would not have martyred him. His wisdom survives even his own wit. For years I have agitated in vain to have universities inscribe over their doorposts his grand admonition: "all bad poetry is sincere."

◈

BIOGRAPHY

◈

OSCAR WILDE
(1854–1900)

❖

Oscar Fingal O'Flahertie Wills Wilde was born in Dublin on October 16, 1854, the son of Dr. William (later Sir William) Wilde, a surgeon, and Jane Francesca Elgee, well known under the pen name Speranza. Wilde studied classics at Trinity College, Dublin (1871–74), and then at Magdalen College, Oxford (1874–78), where in 1878 he won the Newdigate Prize for his poem *Ravenna*. In 1881 Wilde published *Poems*, a volume that was successful enough to lead to a lecture tour in the United States in 1882. In all his public appearances Wilde, who proclaimed himself a disciple of Pater, displayed a flamboyant aestheticism that did much to increase his notoriety.

Wilde returned to the United States in 1883 in order to attend an unsuccessful New York production of his play *Vera*, written the year before. In 1884, after moving to London, he married Constance Lloyd, although shortly afterwards he began to have homosexual affairs. *The Happy Prince and Other Tales*, a volume of fairy tales written for his two sons, appeared in 1888 and was followed by his only novel, *The Picture of Dorian Gray*, which appeared in *Lippincott's Magazine* in 1890 and in book form in 1891. Also in 1891, Wilde's play *The Duchess of Padua* was produced in New York under another title and anonymously, without much success. Wilde's essay "The Soul of Man under Socialism," a plea for artistic freedom, appeared in 1891, as did *Intentions*, containing the critical dialogues "The Decay of Lying" and "The Critic as Artist"; *Lord Arthur Savile's Crime and Other Stories;* and another collection of fairy tales, *The House of Pomegranates.*

Wilde first found theatrical success with his play *Lady Windermere's Fan* (1893), which combined social observation with a witty, epigrammatic style. This formula was pursued successfully in the plays that followed, including *A Woman of No Importance* (1894), *An Ideal Husband* (1899), and *The Importance of Being Earnest* (1899). *Salomé,* published in French in 1893, was translated into English by Lord Alfred Douglas in 1894 and performed in Paris by Sarah Bernhardt in 1896, after being denied a license in England. Lord Alfred, whom Wilde had first met in 1891, was

Wilde's lover, and their relationship so disturbed the Marquess of Queensberry, Lord Alfred's father, that he publicly insulted Wilde on several occasions beginning in 1894. This prompted Wilde to bring a charge of criminal libel against Lord Queensberry, but the suit was dismissed, and Wilde, after two trials, was imprisoned for homosexual offenses in 1895. In prison, where he remained for two years, Wilde wrote a letter to Lord Alfred that was partially published in 1905 as *De Profundis*. It contained his own justification for his conduct. After his release in 1897, Wilde went to France, where he published "The Ballad of Reading Gaol" (1898), inspired by his prison experiences. In exile, he adopted the name Sebastian Melmoth, taken from Charles Robert Maturin's gothic romance *Melmoth the Wanderer*. Wilde died in Paris on November 30, 1900. His *Collected Works* were edited by Robert Ross (12 vols., 1909). His *Letters*, edited by Rupert Hart-Davis, appeared in 1962; a supplementary volume was published in 1985.

❖

PERSONAL

❖

The following extracts present various views of Wilde's character, a number given by his friends, some by acquaintances of varying degree, at least one in which the author claims no personal relationship with Wilde at all. What the extracts have in common is just how difficult it was, and remains for critics today, to justify absolute statements about Wilde's personal qualities. Almost every extract's author feels that he or she has some form of insight into Wilde's character, but those impressions are always specific to a particular meeting and a momentary appreciation of the man at a single point in time. The only author who seems uniformly comfortable in defining Wilde's character is Thomas F. Plowman, the one person quoted here who does not claim a personal reminiscence or acquaintance with Wilde.

This tendency to describe Wilde's personality as revealed during a particular meeting with him is not uncommon. It is no coincidence that Plowman's statements are so self-assured, for anyone who was acquainted with Wilde knew that he was the consummate performer, that just as he brought dramatic characters into being for the stage, so he staged his own personality for various people, at various times, in a variety of ways. Like his novel's antihero, Dorian Gray, Wilde did not understand identity "as a thing simple, permanent, reliable, and of one essence" but as a succession of masks and guises to be put on and taken off as he desired. But, if identity is constantly shifting, how then does a writer critically assess an individual's character? What the majority of writers presented here have pursued is perhaps the only possible course presented them: to capture Wilde at a single moment or in a series of momentary poses. The most intelligent of these authors do not extrapolate from the singular to the general; they recognize that their recollections are unique to only one particular instance of who Wilde was and that this is perhaps the most profound understanding that one might formulate of the man.

Plowman, a few months before the first of the 1895 trials, discusses Wilde's "attitudinised" role as the leader of the "cult" of aestheticism. He describes Wilde's self-promotion as a commodity that the educated classes, in search of the latest shocking fashion, are served up by journalists eager to cash in on an author's celebrity. In contrast to Plowman's assaults on Wilde, journalist Chris Healy's recollections are kind and sympathetic and present both Wilde's wit and "attitude" as counter to the prevailing conventions and fashions of the day.

The next two extracts portray Wilde's closest friends and their reactions to his downfall: The first is a description by Wilfred Scawen Blunt of a conversation he had with Robert ("Robbie") Ross, Wilde's close friend and literary executor, about the author's final days in Paris. The second is Robert Harborough Sherard's memory of the climactic period of Wilde's last trial and his account of the passing of the guilty verdict and the general glee in the aftermath among those who had not personally known Wilde. Despite the fact that these two Roberts were arguably Wilde's closest long-term friends, the way each man portrays his memories is distinctly different. Ross is remembered by Scawen Blunt as being thoughtfully and introspectively saddened by the end of Wilde's life, as he considers the sincerity of his friend's possible conversion to Roman Catholicism. Sherard's reminiscence is a melodrama, and he seems to have cast himself as its hero. It is an extract that highlights the importance for any critical reader of discerning the possible intentions of the author, for Sherard had been attacked for breaking with Wilde, as many of his former friends had done. As Wilde's most prolific biographer in the years immediately following his death, Sherard had the opportunity to favorably rewrite his relationship with Wilde. Has he done so? Certainly the extract presented here suggests at least an overly imaginative and dramatic recollection on Sherard's part.

The final two extracts come from Ford Madox Ford and Katharine Tynan, each a well-known novelist and poet, contemporaries and sometime acquaintances of Wilde. Madox Ford's extract, like Ross's remembrance of Wilde's final days, is unromanticized and honest. He critiques both Wilde's witticisms and his writing but appreciates his scholarly ability and the fact that Wilde's art gave a great deal of pleasure to many people. Tynan's memory of a younger Oscar, before his marriage, is one of vague amusement. She concentrates on his posing and self-publicizing even in those early days of his London career, but, in contrast to Plowman's sneering, she does little more than gently tease Wilde's memory. Her pity for Constance, Wilde's wife-to-be, is more seriously presented in light of his later downfall and the amount Constance would suffer by association with her husband.

No one extract can absolutely gainsay another in the depiction of Wilde, even though each suggests a very different picture of the man. The fact that these attitudes could simultaneously coexist testifies to the insight of Robbie Ross when he said that one could never be sure of Wilde. Wilde had attempted to turn his own life into a work of art and had said that, "A truth in art is that whose contradictory is also true." Such attitudes are precisely those that should be kept in mind by any critic seeking to define Oscar Wilde's character: Each attempt at a definition of his identity should be particular and every interpretation contingent.

THOMAS F. PLOWMAN "THE AESTHETES: THE STORY OF A NINETEENTH-CENTURY CULT" (1895)

The following extract, written a few months before Wilde's trial and subsequent incarceration, typifies the general public's view of Wilde's character, art, and lifestyle. Thomas Plowman barely conceals his sneering tone and belief that Wilde adopted an "attitude" for vulgar financial reasons and that the journalistic marketplace encouraged such behavior as it made money along with the writer it helped to publicize and popularize. The educated classes are described by Plowman as foolishly following the latest fad, delighting in the shock value of Wilde's views. The suggestion at the conclusion of the extract is that Wilde was fully aware of his power to entertain these "smart people" who were so eager to listen to him and quite knowingly used them to advance himself before the general public via the press. Plowman describes the aestheticism proposed by Wilde as a "cult," pronouncing Wilde an artistic charlatan and his admiring followers dupes.

Mr. Wilde laid himself out to play a certain *role,* and when he attitudinised he did it sufficiently well to make it pay, and to induce the world to take him seriously. When he was interviewed by newspaper correspondents his remarks made what is professionally known as "good copy," because he usually said something that startled a serious world by its audacity. When, after crossing the Atlantic, he responded to an inquiry on the subject by expressing his disappointment with the "mighty ocean," persons of a superior type, who expect poetic rhapsodies on such an occasion, in accordance with precedent, were naturally shocked.

He set conventionality at defiance in other respects, and in his lectures expressed some revolutionary sentiments with reference to modern costume, from an art point of view. He had a good word to say for knee-breeches and silk stockings, but spoke disrespectfully of coats and trousers, and more in sorrow than in anger of the chimney-pot hat, which he did not regard as "the thing of beauty" referred to by the poet as "a joy for ever." He even had the hardihood to insinuate that the nineteenth-century Englishman in his "Sunday best" was not, from a spectacular point of view, comparable to the ancient Greek in his temple get-up. As neither the fashionable tailors nor Mrs. Grundy could endorse anything so heterodox, it need hardly be said that he made but few converts to his views on costume, and we go on "just in the old sweet way" in the matter of outward apparel. The freedom with which he enunciated extreme opinions, such as these, induced the polite world, or, as we prefer to term them nowadays, the "smart people," who are always on the look-out for something piquant, to flock to his lectures in order to listen to the next dreadful thing he would say; and this must have been very much in consonance with Mr. Wilde's expectations and desires.

—Thomas F. Plowman, "The Aesthetes:
The Story of a Nineteenth-Century Cult,"
Pall Mall Magazine, January 1895, pp. 41–42

CHRIS HEALY (1904)

Chris Healy was a young Irish poet and journalist working as a freelance correspondent in Paris when Wilde left prison and then England for France and Italy. Wilde spent much of his time in the French capital, and it was there that Healy became acquainted with him. On the Continent, Wilde lived under the assumed name of Sebastian Melmoth, the first name recollecting the martyred saint, the second an allusion to the God-cursed, gothic antihero of his great-uncle Charles Maturin's novel *Melmoth the Wanderer*. Wilde wrote to his friend Robert Ross in 1898 that at the time he was seeing few other people apart from Healy, his young Irish compatriot.

In *Confessions of a Journalist*, Healy fondly describes his friendship with Wilde and champions the disgraced writer's memory. There is a sense of the young Healy's pride from the opening line of the following extract when he includes himself as one of "the few" who could appreciate Wilde's character and mind. He is no sycophant to Wilde's memory, however: He describes Wilde's homosexuality as a "most terrible and loathsome" type of madness. But it is clear that his recollections of Wilde are of a kind, generous, and rare individual, a great artist, and a cultivated gentleman. He remarks several times on how Wilde has suffered, essentially claiming that he was made a martyr for his "sins" by "the many" from whom Healy has already distanced himself at the beginning of the extract. If Wilde had suffered physically from his time in prison, the conversation relayed in this extract makes it apparent that his wit and intellectual verve remained undiminished.

To the many Wilde was an unspeakable person, but to the few he was an accomplished scholar and gentleman, suffering from one of the most terrible and loathsome forms of insanity, which two years of prison life increased rather than diminished. I met him in Paris a few weeks after he finally left England, and his appearance was burnt in on my memory. A tall, stalwart figure, with a face scored with suffering and a mistaken life. The gray, wearied eyes, the mocking curves of the mobile mouth, reminded me of Charles Reade's description of Thomas of Sarranza at the time that he sat in the Fisherman's Seat—'a *gentilhomme blase*, a high-bred and highly-cultivated gentleman who had done, and said, and seen, and known everything, and whose body was nearly worn out.'

Wilde was then living in the Rue des Beaux Arts, under the name of Sebastian Melmoth. He invited me to lunch, and we had dejeuner at a little restaurant on the Boulevard St. Michel, where for over two hours he talked with the same delightful insouciance which had characterized him in his best days. Wilde detested coarse language or coarse conduct, and I remember him moving his chair away from the vicinity of some students who, with their Mimis and Marcelles, were talking in a strain that would have made Rabelais blush. He talked lightly about his trial, but his face lighted up with savage indignation when he spoke of his prison treatment. Of one prison official he said: 'He had the eyes of a ferret, the body of an ape, and the soul of a rat.' The chaplains he characterized as 'the silliest of God's silly sheep,' and gave an instance of the kind of reading they select for the prisoners under their charge. A man had been sentenced to seven years' imprisonment, six months of which was to be endured in solitary confinement.

The book served out to him by the chaplain at ---- Prison was 'Sermons Delivered at ---- Prison to Prisoners under Sentence of Death.' I had had the advantage of reading *The Ballad of Reading Gaol* in manuscript some days before I met the author, and I asked him whether he intended to write further in the same vein.

'Do not ask me about it!' Wilde said with a sigh. 'It is the cry of Marsyas, not the song of Apollo. I have probed the depths of most of the experiences of life, and I have come to the conclusion that we are meant to suffer. There are moments when life takes you, like a tiger, by the throat, and it was when I was in the depths of suffering that I wrote my poem. The man's face will haunt me till I die.'

The conversation drifted on to Aubrey Beardsley, who was then on the point of becoming a Catholic.

'I never guessed,' said Wilde, 'when I invented Aubrey Beardsley, that there was an atom of aught but pagan feeling in him.'

I happened to mention something that Herr Max Nordau had told me the day before on the subject of 'The Degenerates,' and on Nordau's firm belief that all men of genius were mad.

'I quite agree with Dr. Nordau's assertion that all men of genius are insane,' said Wilde, 'but Dr. Nordau forgets that all sane people are idiots.'

He leaned back in his chair, lit a cigarette, and gazed reflectively at the beautiful scarab ring on his finger. 'I shall start working again, and trust to the generosity of the English people to judge it on its merits, and apart from their Philistine prejudices against myself. I do not acknowledge that I have ever been wrong . . . only society is stronger than I. Should the English people refuse my work, then I shall cross to America, a great country which has always treated me kindly. I have always been drawn towards America, not only because it has produced a very great poet—its only one—in Walt Whitman, but because the American people are capable of the highest things in art, literature, and life.'

'Do you not care for Longfellow, then?'

'Longfellow is a great poet only for those who never read poetry. But America is great because it is the only country in the world where slang is borrowed from the highest literature. I remember some years ago, when I was travelling out West, I was passing by a store when a cowboy galloped past. The man with me said: "Last night that fellow painted the town red." It was a fine phrase, and familiar. Where had I heard it? I could not remember, but the same afternoon, when I was taken to see the public buildings—the only ones in this place were the gaols and cemeteries—I was shown a condemned cell where a prisoner, who had been sentenced to death, was calmly smoking a cigarette and reading *The Divine Comedy* of Dante in the original. Then I saw that Dante had invented the phrase "painting the town red." Do you remember the scene where Dante, led by Virgil, comes to the cavernous depths of the place swept by a mighty wind, where are confined those who have been the prey of their passions? Two pale faces arise from the mist—the faces of Francesca da Rimini and her lover. "Who art thou?" cries Dante in alarm, and Francesca replies sadly: "We are those who painted the world red with our sin." It is only a great country which can turn the greatest literature into colloquial phrases.' . . .

The end of his meteoric career is too sad to be dealt with here. Suffice it to say that, if his terrible mania made him sin in the eyes of the world, he suffered no less terribly. Apart from this side of his character, he had a rare delicacy in the things of this world, and his remark that Zola was a writer of immoral books, to which my 'Mawworm' critic objected, was made in all sincerity. Those who really knew him made due allowance on his behalf, ignoring the maniac who had fallen under the ban of English displeasure, and recking only of the rare artist, the accomplished scholar, the greatest sonneteer in the world of poetry since the days of Rossetti and John Keats, and the kindly gentleman whose heart was a mine of generosity and good nature. May his soul rest in peace and his sins be forgiven him!

—Chris Healy, *Confessions of a Journalist*, 1904, pp. 131–138

WILFRED SCAWEN BLUNT (1905)

Wilfred Scawen Blunt was an English poet, political essayist, and polemicist. In this extract from his diaries, he describes a conversation he had with Robert Ross, Wilde's closest friend and his literary executor. It depicts Ross's impressions of Wilde's difficult time in prison, the writing of his essay *De Profundis*, and his sad physical decline after his release. The Roman Catholic Ross describes Wilde's flirtation with conversion and his deathbed baptism into the Roman Catholic Church. Blunt highlights Ross's portrayal of Wilde's "artificial temperament," his variable sincerities, and the difficulty even his closest and oldest friend had in simply understanding Wilde. Scawen Blunt largely refrains from passing any personal comments since he is receiving his information secondhand from Ross. Ross, however, has a very firm conviction about the complicated nature of Wilde's personality and temperament: He states simply that "It was difficult to be sure about him."

Yesterday I saw (Robert) Ross, Oscar Wilde's friend, who was with him in his last hours. I was curious to know about these and he told me everything. Ross is a good honest fellow as far as I can judge, and stood by Oscar when all had abandoned him. He used to go to him in prison, being admitted on an excuse of legal business, for Ross managed some of Mrs. Wilde's affairs while her husband was shut up. He told me Oscar was very hardly treated during his first year, as he was a man of prodigious appetite and required more food than the prison allowance gave him, also he suffered from an outbreak of old symptoms and was treated as a malingerer when he complained of it. Ross's representation got attention paid to these things, and in the last eight months of his imprisonment, Wilde had books and writing materials in abundance and so was able to write his *De Profundis*. I asked him how much of this poem was sincere. He said, 'As much as possible in a man of Oscar's artificial temperament. While he was writing he was probably sincere, but his "style" was always in his mind. It was difficult to be sure about him. Sometimes when I called he was hysterical, at other times laughing. When Oscar came out of prison he had the idea of becoming a Catholic, and he consulted me about it, for you know I am a Catholic. I did not believe in his sincerity and told him if he really meant it, to go to a priest, and I discouraged him from anything hasty in the matter. As a fact, he had forgotten all about it in a week, only from time to time he used to chaff me as one standing in the way of his salvation. I would willingly have helped him if I had thought him in earnest, but I did not fancy religion being made ridiculous by him. I used to say that if it came to his dying I would bring a priest to him, not before. I am not at all a moral man, but I had my feeling on this point and so the matter remained between us. After he had been nearly a year out of prison he took altogether to drink, and the last two years of his life were sad to witness. I was at Rome when I heard that he was dying and returned at once to Paris and found him in the last stage of meningitis. It is a terrible disease for the bystanders, though they say the sufferer himself is unconscious. He had only a short time to live, and I remembered my promise and got a priest to come to him. I asked him if he would consent to see him, and he held up his hand, for he could not speak. When the priest, an Englishman, Cuthbert Dunn, came to him he asked him whether he wished to be received and put the usual questions, and again Oscar held up his hand, but he was in no condition to make a confession nor could he say a word. On this sign, however, Dunn allowing him the benefit of the doubt, gave him conditional baptism, and afterwards extreme unction but not communion. He was never able to speak and we do not know whether he was altogether conscious. I did this for the sake of my own conscience and the promise I had made.' Wilde's wife died a year after he left prison. She would have gone to see him at Paris but he had already taken to drink, and Ross did not encourage her to do so. Ross made £800 by the *De Profundis*. He had intended to pay off Oscar's Paris debts with £400 of it and devote the rest to the use of the boys, but just as he was going to do this the whole sum was claimed by the bankruptcy court and the affair is not yet settled.

—Wilfred Scawen Blunt, *My Diaries* (entry for
November 16, 1905), 1920, vol. 2, pp. 125–126

ROBERT H. SHERARD (1905)

Robert Sherard was an English journalist and poet, the great-grandson of William Wordsworth. He was the prolific biographer of Wilde in the early twentieth century and one of his closest friends, until anger at Wilde's continued same-sex relations after his release from prison caused a break between the two men. Sherard had been working desperately for a reconciliation between Wilde and his wife, Constance, up until that point. In the copy of *De Profundis* sent to Sherard, Wilde wrote an inscription expressing sadness, and perhaps resentment, because of this estrangement from his erstwhile friend.

The following extract gives a personal and detailed account of the last days leading up to Wilde's conviction in the Old Bailey courtroom. Considering that Sherard had broken with Wilde before the latter's death, it is impossible to assess just how much faith should be placed in Sherard's account of his feelings, as they are related here. There is reason to doubt his despair and pain so dramatically, indeed so melodramatically, described; but this typifies the problem with so many people who wrote of Wilde after his death. Those who had chosen to ignore Wilde or break with him upon his release from prison for whatever reason would often be the same individuals claiming to have been closest to him, members of his inner circle, the few who never betrayed him. Sherard claims to feel as if he is being lashed as each "Guilty" verdict is announced. He maintains he had to be held back from leaping up and causing a scene as his condemned friend was led away and says of himself that he was close to collapse as he left the courtroom after the sentencing.

Sherard states that he was the only friend of Wilde's prescient enough to have held little hope of his receiving an acquittal. His disgust with the establishment's hypocrisy is evident in the detestation he feels for the male prostitutes ("The Evidence") who perjured themselves to convict his friend, their laughing and smoking during the jury's deliberations and after the trial ended. Sherard says that only one of nine guilty of a crime was sentenced in the courtroom that day. The general public is described as cavorting with glee when the verdict was announced outside the court, behaving much as the mob might have done at a nobleman's execution during the French Revolution. They dance an ugly farandole and behave with "mad joy" in the muddy street.

The conclusion of the extract describes Sherard's difficult visit the same evening to the French writer Alphonse Daudet (Sherard had published his biography only the year before). The Frenchman is pleased with the verdict and displays no sympathy for the downfall of a fellow writer. Sherard dines luxuriously with Daudet and others that evening but claims the food tastes terrible as he imagines Wilde's prison fare. The suggestion for a story about a hermit seems to be Sherard's insinuation that he can no longer abide becoming friends with those who will cause him pain: whether this is a statement about his future relationship with Wilde or with Daudet is unclear. Sherard certainly sees himself as

being the misanthrope of the title, who has adopted such a state simply
because he loves others so much: he cannot be happy in a world where
his own love is transformed into suffering. It is a fittingly melodramatic
conclusion to the extract and expresses, unfortunately, a not uncommon
sentiment in those who wrote of Wilde's downfall and of their feelings at
the time.

The day of the trial dawned as a day of relief to all of us in Oakley Street, but to
none more so than to my unhappy friend. It had never entered my mind to
be present at the Old Bailey, where he was to be exposed to such humiliations.
We breakfasted together, and afterwards one of the men who had found his
bail came to escort him to surrender. This man was bright and cheerful. "I
have a nice carriage to drive there in," he said, "and I have retained a nice
room near the Old Bailey, to which he can retire during the intervals."

I remember saying, "You would have done much better to retain a nice
room for him on the Calle del Sol in Madrid." I never hoped for a moment
that the trial would be otherwise than fatal to him.

I have no recollection of the impressions of those days, save that they were
days of shifting hopes and fears. The town was placarded with his name; and
one night, alluding to this, I said, "Well, you have got your name before
the public at last." He laughed and said, "Nobody can pretend now not to
have heard of it."

I did not read the papers, and all I knew of the progress of the trial was
what I gathered from the announcements on the posters and what little
was said in Oakley Street when the accused returned home. But there was
nothing to encourage me, and what I dreaded most was the effect he would
produce when placed in person in the witness-box. I feared his bent for
flippancy and paradox would dispose the jury against him; but what disturbed
me most was, that he was obviously in no state of health to defend himself
effectively. His nerve was all gone, and I feared that his physical collapse would
be construed as a sign of the consciousness of guilt. He himself dreaded this
ordeal. "I shall break down," he said, the evening before. "I know that I shall
break down." I understood, however, from those that were present, that he
acquitted himself with courage and dignity.

There was one evening when everybody was glad, and when I was
pointed at as a prophet of evil and a foolish counsellor. It was the evening of
the day on which the judge had contemptuously pitchforked back on to the
dungheap, from which it had exuded, a certain part of the Evidence.

On the eve of the fatal last day, however, everybody seemed resigned for the worst. He was very fine, and I admired him greatly. His old serenity had come back to him. His face was calm; all traces of nervousness had gone; there was a manliness in his bearing which years of self-indulgence had masked till then. He spent his last evening in arranging for his mother's needs in the event of a forced separation, and disposed of the few trinkets of which he had not been plundered, as souvenirs to his friends. He retired early, taking leave of those assembled in turn. I put my arms round his neck and embraced him, and I said, "God bless you, Oscar," for I thought that I should never see him again. Apart from my conduct, which was prompted by my great sorrow and a weakness of nerve which bordered on hysteria, that farewell-taking was not lacking in dignity. And the cruelty of it was, that but for the charge against him, his attitude that night in the face of imminent danger would have authorised his friends to proclaim the man a hero.

I had thought that I should never see him again. But as that dreadful Saturday dragged on, the impulse grew stronger and stronger within me to go to him, so as to be with him at the end. In the afternoon then, meeting Ernest Dowson, I asked him to accompany me to the Old Bailey. We drove there, and as we alighted in front of the court-house, a shout arose from the rabble that thronged the street, "Here are some more aristocrats! Here are some more of them!"

I said to Dowson, as we passed through the doorway which leads into the little yard between the court-house and Newgate, "That shout explains that much of the popular execration of our friend proceeds from class hatred. He represents the aristocrat, poor fellow, to them, and they are exulting in the downfall of an aristocrat."

We found a few friends in the passage from which judge and barristers by one staircase, and witnesses by another, reach the court-room, and I heard that after a deadly summing-up the jury had retired. There could be no hope of a favourable verdict. I was fully prepared for this news, but none the less it came as a shock. A friend diverted my thoughts by pointing to something on the other side of the yard—a something that was seated on a bench,—a multiple something that was giggling and chatting and smoking cigarettes. It was The Evidence. After awhile, a friend came out of the Court and told me that if I cared to come in, there was a place for me. I entered, and found the room by no means as crowded as I had expected, and amongst those present very few faces that I recognised. My friend was sitting in the dock, covering a sheet of paper with innumerable Deltas. I saluted him, but he only acknowledged my greeting with the faintest inclination of the head. I sat down on the bench behind the counsel for the Crown, and next to a barrister who was a friend of mine. He whispered to me that all chance was gone. Still, the jury were a long time in discussion, and each minute strengthened hope. After a long while we heard a bell, an usher came bustling in, and a great silence fell upon the buzzing Court. It was the silence of a beast of prey which, to seize its victim, opens a yawning mouth, and perforce suspends its roar. But it was a false alarm. The jury had sent a question to the judge.

"That means an acquittal," said the Treasury counsel.

"No, no, no," said Sir Edward, shaking his head.

"Thus do they compliment each other," I whispered to my neighbour. The Treasury counsel overheard my whisper, and turned round, with a mighty face suffused with joviality. It was like a sudden sun in a very evil mist, and it quite cheered me to see that my friend's adversary was such a pleasant gentleman. And still the minutes went by. "There may be another disagreement," said my friend. But whilst he yet spoke the die had been cast.

I noticed that the judge's hand shook as in a palsy as he arranged his papers on the desk. As to the jury, a glance at their faces was sufficient. Six questions had been put to them, and "Guilty" was the answer to each. Such was the foreman's enthusiasm of conviction, that to the question "Is that the verdict of you all?" he answered with another "Guilty,"—a piece of overweight—a bonus to public opinion. I had laid my head down on my arms at the first "Guilty" and groaned, and each fresh condemnation, like a lash on my back, drew from me an exclamation of pain.

I could not look at my friend. Amongst all those eyes turned on him in that moment, he should not notice mine. But I looked at him when the judge was passing sentence, and the face is one I shall never forget. It was flushed purple, the eyes protruded, and over all was an expression of extreme horror. When the judge had finished speaking, and whilst a whirr of satisfaction buzzed through the Court, Wilde, who had recovered himself, said, "And I? May I say nothing, my lord?" But the judge made no answer— only an impatient sign with his hand to the warders. I jumped up, to do what or say what I cannot fancy, but was pulled down by my friend the barrister. "You'll do no good," he said, "and you'll be sent to Holloway."

Warders touched my poor friend on the shoulder. He shuddered and gave one wild look round the Court. Then he turned and lumbered forward to the head of the stairs which led to the bottomless pit. He was swept down and disappeared.

As I staggered down the steps to leave the court-house, I dimly heard the cries of exultation which those crowding down with me were uttering. But this fiendish joy in the ruin of a life was to be impressed upon me still more vividly. For when the verdict and the sentence on 'the aristocrat' reached the rabble in Old Bailey, men and women joined hands and danced an ungainly farandole, where ragged petticoats and yawning boots flung up the London mud in *feu de joie,* and the hideous faces were distorted with savage triumph. I stood and watched this dance of death for a few minutes, regretting that Veretschagin was not by my side; and whilst I was standing there, I saw The Evidence, still laughing and smoking cigarettes, being driven off in cabs. And I said to Dowson, "This is a trial in which, out of nine people incriminated, eight have been admitted to act as Queen's Evidence." Then we walked on—I as in a dream.

That evening I went to see Daudet. He said, "This is a fine country. I admire a country where justice is administered as it is here, as is shown by to-day's verdict and sentence."

I said nothing, for there was nothing to say, and there was nothing to do but to bend under the inevitable. I dined with the Daudets and a Lord Somebody that night, and the dinner was a luxurious one. But every mouthful I took had a strange savour, for I was thinking of what poor Wilde might at that moment be scooping out of a greasy pannikin with a wooden spoon, and the thought flavoured all the sauces of that dinner.

I know little of his prison life, for I never spoke to him on the subject after his release, and what I do know is from hearsay only, but it appears that that first evening in Wandsworth Gaol was to him one of terrible suffering— indeed, that he revolted when he was told to enter a filthy bath in which other prisoners had preceded him. But his experiences cannot have been worse than I pictured them.

Daudet was very kind to me all the evening; and when I was leaving, he invited me to come early on the morrow, so that we might have a long time at our book; "For," he said, "it is in work only that you will find consolation."

"Ah, yes," I answered; "but when the mainspring is broken and one can work no longer—"

It was on the following day, I think, that I said to him, "I want to write a story, *maltre,* which I shall call "The Misanthrope by Philanthropy,"—the story of a man who becomes a hermit because he has a tender and a susceptible heart, and wishes to escape the certain suffering which would fall to his lot, if he lived in the world, and formed attachments and grew fond of friends."

—Robert H. Sherard, from *Oscar Wilde: The Story of an Unhappy Friendship,* 1905, pp. 183–194

FORD MADOX FORD (1911)

Ford Madox Ford was an English novelist, poet, critic, and the editor of *The Transatlantic Review* and *The English Review*, two journals fundamental to the development of literary modernism. As a modernist, it is unsurprising that Madox Ford was not overly enthusiastic about Wilde's literary output, as is evident in the following extract. The acceptance of *fin de siècle* aestheticism was not only irreversibly qualified due to Wilde's incarceration but also because of the growing interest in modernism.

However, Madox Ford's statements on Wilde are remarkably honest and balanced. He makes it clear that despite his personal dislike for the man, his considered opinion is that the famous wit is nothing of the sort. Madox Ford expresses his amazement that Wilde might be thought an artist of the first caliber by anyone. Still the author here sees that there still exists much to admire in Wilde: He recognizes that Wilde's conversation gave pleasure to many, as did his poetry and plays. Madox Ford considers Wilde to have been an accomplished scholar, and he believes that Wilde's trial was of no public benefit. Madox Ford then goes even further, claiming that Wilde had been pushed to the actions and behaviors leading to his downfall by those claiming to be his friends, those same individuals who would abandon him and betray him after his arrest.

The story relayed at the beginning of the extract makes Madox Ford's evenhandedness and honest sympathy even more apparent. He recognizes that Wilde's torture at the hands of the students of Montmartre might have been eased if he had intervened, and he knows in leaving the café so abruptly that he did not act the role of a hero. He does not attempt, like those "shameful," self-styled friends who would desert Wilde, to portray himself as anything other than what he is. He sees Wilde, despite his own opinions of the man and his art, as a "notable" and "tragic figure" for whom he feels, if not pity, at least a forthright compassion.

The conclusion of the extract suggests just how difficult it was, and would continue to be, for a literary critic (and Madox Ford was one of the foremost of his day) to position Wilde's aestheticism within the literary canon. The gentleman leaving the museum baffles Madox Ford by seeing Wilde as a proponent of Pre-Raphaelitism, an artistic movement that had seen its heyday pass several decades before, and of which Madox Ford's own grandfather had been a leading light. Wilde is "unrecognizable" as a member of this movement, but Madox Ford does not suggest precisely where he believes Wilde's aestheticism *does* belong or how it might be defined in any other way than flippantly.

Wilde himself I met only in his later years. I remember being at a garden party of the Bishop of London, and hearing behind me a conversation so indelicate that I could not resist turning around. Oscar Wilde, very fat, with the remainder of young handsomeness—even of young beauty—was talking to a lady. It would be more precise to say that the lady was talking to Wilde, for it was certainly she who supplied the indelicacies in their conversation, for as I knew Wilde he had a singularly cleanly tongue.

But I found him exceedingly difficult to talk to, and I only once remember hearing him utter one of his brilliancies. This was at a private view of the New Gallery. Some one asked Wilde if he were not going to the soiree of the O. P. Club. Wilde, who at that time had embroiled himself with that organization, replied: "No. Why, I should be like a poor lion in a den of savage Daniels."

I saw him once or twice afterwards in Paris, where he was, I think, rather shamefully treated by the younger denizens of Montmartre and of the Quartier Latin. I remember him as, indeed, a tragic figure, seated at a table in a little cabaret, lachrymosely drunk, and being tormented by an abominable gang of young students of the four arts.

Wilde possessed a walking-stick with an ivory head, to which he attached much affection—and, indeed, in his then miserable poverty it was an object of considerable intrinsic value. Prowling about the same cabaret was one of those miserable wrecks of humanity, a harmless, parasitic imbecile, called Bibi Latouche. The young students were engaged in persuading poor Wilde that this imbecile was a dangerous malefactor. Bibi was supposed to have taken a fancy to Wilde's walking-stick, and the young men persuaded the poet that if he did not surrender this treasure he would be murdered on his way home through the lonely streets. Wilde cried and protested.

I do not know that I acted any heroic part in the matter. I was so disgusted that I went straight out of the cafe, permanently cured of any taste for Bohemianism that I may ever have possessed. Indeed, I have never since been able to see a student, with his blue beret, his floating cloak, his floating tie, and his youthful beard, without a feeling of aversion.

One of Wilde's French intimates of that date assured me, and repeated with the utmost earnestness and many asseverations, that he was sure Wilde only sinned *par pure snobisme,* and in order to touch the Philistine on the raw. Of this I am pretty well satisfied, just as I am certain that such a trial as that of Wilde was a lamentable error of public policy on the part of the police. He should have been given his warning, and have been allowed to escape across the Channel. That any earthly good could come of the trial, no one, I think, would be so rash as to advance. I did not like Wilde, his works seemed to me derivative and of no importance, his humour thin and mechanical, and I am lost in amazement at the fact that in Germany and to some extent in France, Wilde should be considered a writer of enormous worth. Nevertheless, I cannot help thinking that his fate was infinitely more bitter than anything he could have deserved. As a scholar he was worthy of the greatest respect. His conversation, though it did not appeal to me, gave, as I can well believe, immense pleasure to innumerable persons; so did his plays, so did his verse. Into his extravagances he was pushed by the quality of his admirers, who demanded always more and more follies; when they had pushed him to his fall, they very shamefully deserted this notable man.

On the afternoon when the sentence against Wilde had been pronounced, I met Dr. Garnett on the steps of the British Museum. He said gravely: "This is the death-blow to English poetry." I looked at him in amazement, and he continued: "The only poets we have are the Pre-Raphaelites, and this will cast so much odium upon them that the habit of reading poetry will die out in England."

I was so astonished that I laughed out loud. I had hardly imagined that Wilde could be called a Pre-Raphaelite at all. Indeed, it was only because of the confusion that existed between Pre-Raphaelism and Estheticism that the name ever became attached to this group of poets. Pre-Raphaelism as it existed in the forties and fifties was a sort of Realism inspired by high moral purpose.

Estheticism, which originated with Burne-Jones and Morris, was a movement that concerned itself with idealizing anything that was mediaeval. It may be symbolized by the words, "long necks and pomegranates." Wilde carried this ideal one stage further. He desired to live upon the smell of a lily. I do not know that he ever did, but I know that he was in the habit of sending to young ladies whom he admired a single lily flower, carefully packed in cotton-wool. And the cry from the austere realism of my grandfather's picture of *Work,* or Holman Hunt's *Saviour in the Temple,* was so far that I may well be pardoned for not recognizing Wilde at all under the mantle of a *soi-disant* Pre-Raphaelite.

—Ford Madox Ford, *Ancient Lights and
Certain New Reflections,* 1911, pp. 150–153

KATHARINE TYNAN (1913)

Katharine Tynan was an Irish novelist and poet and a lifelong and close acquaintance of her fellow and famous Irish poet William Butler Yeats. In this extract, Tynan recalls her first introduction to Wilde, made by Wilde's own mother, but also dwells on her memories of Constance Lloyd, the woman who would become Wilde's wife. Tynan clearly sympathizes with Constance's future suffering and contrasts it to the expectations of those gathered who envied her relationship with the young, famous poet, the toast of London at the time. This is perhaps why Tynan describes Wilde as both a somewhat ludicrous caricature (Bunthorne, the foppish poet in Gilbert and Sullivan's popular comic opera *Patience*) as well as a figure who suggested a certain cruelty (the infamous French revolutionaries Marat and Robespierre). She also emphasizes Wilde's desire to be the center of attention, the lighting in the room set to fall on him in conversation. His "posing" is also central to Tynan's reminiscence: his entrance to the party in semidarkness, his appearing like the photographs in which he wears occasionally outlandish attire, his staged position on the divan, the positioning of his own pictures around the room showcasing his unashamed and deliberate self-publicity, and finally his self-reflexive statement about young, Irish geniuses being plentiful, the presumed suggestion being that the London literary scene's desire for them was triggered by an initial appreciation of Wilde.

Presently came Oscar, and growing accustomed to the darkness one could see how like he was to the photographs of him which were all about the room, full-face, half-face, three-quarter face; full-length, half-length, three-quarter length; head only; in a fur coat; in a college gown; in ordinary clothes. He came and stood under the limelight so to speak, in the centre of the room. There was some sort of divan or ottoman there on which Miss Fortescue and he sat for a while in conversation. The shaded light had been arranged so as to fall upon them. With him had come in the girl who was afterwards to have the irreparable misfortune to be his wife, poor picturesque pretty Constance Lloyd, dressed all in brown, a long brown cloak, a wide brown velvet hat with a plume. How charming it is in one's memory now that feminine fashions have reached the nadir of hideousness. She was a delicate charming creature, little fitted to endure the terrible fate that was to be hers. At the time, doubtless many people thought her fate enviable.

One was brought up to Oscar and introduced. Then and always I found him pleasant, kind and interested. My impression of his looks was of an immense fat face, somewhat pendulous cheeks, and a shock of dark hair, a little like the poet Bunthorne perhaps—a little also like Marat or Robespierre. I found nothing in him of the witty impertinence other people record him.

I remember that Hannah Lynch's introduction to him was in this way. Lady Wilde said: "This is Miss Hannah Lynch, Oscar: a young Irish genius." Oscar: "Are not young Irish geniuses as plentiful as blackberries?"

—Katharine Tynan, *Twenty-five Years:*
Reminisce, 1913, pp. 149–150

◆

GENERAL

◆

Wilde's celebrity for more than a decade in London's social and artistic circles—paired with his fame abroad in France, the United States, and his homeland of Ireland—made his very public and publicized downfall in 1895 the type of dramatic event more likely to be read about in today's tabloids. Virtually overnight, Wilde's plays, some of the dramatic "bestsellers" of their time, were removed from theaters, as was his name from theater posters. His books suffered a collapse in sales. The jealousy and rumor that had dogged Wilde for much of the preceding decade were fully expressed in the glee with which the general public greeted his sentence.

The following extracts, arranged chronologically, detail the rise and fall of Wilde in social and critical opinion. Each extract attempts in various ways to provide an understanding of the man, his art, and the relationship of his character to his aesthetic philosophy. The incredibly varied responses to Wilde are not so much a matter of when each was written—although changes in literary tastes and values and the rise of modernism certainly contributed to varying appreciations of Wilde's art—but are rather testament to the complexity of the man himself.

Much of the critical disagreement revolves around just what manner of man and artist Wilde was and recognizes, in his aesthetic philosophy of "the truth of masks," the fundamental difficulty in accurately defining and representing his identity. When Wilde suggested that the artist was being true to his constantly shifting perspectives and to his art when he adopted various personalities and guises, the question of what lay behind each mask became virtually impossible to answer. What is the relationship between a series of personas, impossible to define as or assemble into a single identity, and the art produced by those same personalities? All of the authors included in this section—some close friends of Wilde's, some his critical enemies from each side of the Atlantic, still others younger critics working from hearsay and legend—attempt to identify Wilde along with the value and the relationship of the man and his art.

The first extract is a vitriolic attack on the young Wilde, newly arrived on the literary and social scene in London, but here reviewed as he steps ashore for his American tour. Wilde's influence on American taste was, of course, much less than his effect on England's, but Ambrose Bierce's comments summarize, if in extreme form, the common attitude held by the "man in the street" when confronted with Wilde's mannered conversation and appearance. The next three extracts are written by close acquaintances of Wilde's who knew him before his prison sentence, and each of whom, in different ways, owed much of their own literary success at the time to the artistic milieu that Wilde had almost singlehandedly created. A young W.B. Yeats, Arthur Symons, and Max Beerbohm treat Wilde and his art much more sympathetically and sensitively than Bierce, although it would be extraordinarily difficult to have done otherwise.

The critical appraisals by Wilfrid Leadman, J. Comyns Carr, and St. John Hankin, written in the middle of the first decade of the twentieth century, present the beginnings of Wilde's rehabilitation within the literary world. Leadman discusses Wilde's homosexuality and conviction, as many critics would do in the following years, but is notable for calling for a consideration of Wilde's art uncolored by his life. The relationship between Wilde's life and his work was, and still is, of fundamental significance to Wildean critics, however, and seemingly was to Wilde, who believed he had put his genius not into his art but into his life. Comyns Carr and Hankin offer contrasting views of Wilde's abilities as a dramatist: The former critic favorably appreciates Wilde's dramatic touch, while the latter, writing as a proponent of the "New Drama" of the early twentieth century, sees in Wilde a wasted talent.

The three extracts that follow deal in various ways with Wilde's morality and the treatment he suffered at the hands of the English public. The first extract is written by Alfred Douglas, upon the publication of Wilde's *Complete Works,* and is in equal measure a eulogy to Wilde's genius and a corrosive assault on the critics Douglas despises for now lining up to praise Wilde. G.K. Chesterton's commentary on Wilde's art and character cleverly combines the critical positions of those who see Wilde as an artist of worth and those who see him as a charlatan. Chesterton suggests that it is about time that Wilde was considered simply as a man of letters rather than remembered for his prison sentence and crime.

James Joyce's thoughts on Wilde are those of a fellow Irishman and portray Wilde as a scapegoat for England's own sins. Wilde's "Irishness" is a critically important subject to consider. It was a topic that, until relatively recently, only his fellow Irishmen tended to discuss. Where the earlier extract in this volume written by Yeats, four years before Wilde's downfall, is amusing and sees England as a nation of humorless Puritans, Joyce writing almost two decades later catalyzes the righteous anger still felt by many over Wilde's incarceration. Yeats's comments in retrospect seem almost a warning of what lies in store for Wilde; Joyce's view of Wilde as both a homosexual and an Irish martyr to English late-Victorian hypocrisy is still a critical commonplace today.

The next four extracts were written in the second decade of the twentieth century and reveal how critical opinion was still divided over the worth of Wilde's art within literary history. The American Lewis Shanks, sympathetic to more modern, formalistic tendencies in art, is generally dismissive of Wilde's work, and, like Bierce thirty years before, although in a much more balanced vein, sees Wilde's aestheticism as being whimsical and generally forgettable. The next extract by the critic Archibald Henderson shows how Wilde's conviction still existed as a dilemma for many critics interested in the "morality" of art and the relationship between the personal and creative life of Wilde. Arthur Ransome analyzes the three "areas" of Wilde's legacy: the legend of his life, his conversation, and his works, and how each might be critically appreciated in the future. Ransome's extract, written in 1912, reveals a sensitive appreciation of Wilde's readmittance into public and critical discourse. Holbrook Jackson's chapter on Wilde from the influential book *The Eighteen Nineties* begins by recognizing the continuing confusion and disagreement among critics as to Wilde's literary place and the value of his work. Jackson writes persuasively that Wilde's life simply cannot be divorced from his texts, for the author himself saw both as being modes of artistic expression. By detailing developments in Wilde's art and life, Jackson makes a convincing argument for their necessarily mutual examination in understanding Wilde, both his character and his aesthetic. Jackson's method is that which is still most often employed by critics today.

The final extract is written ten years after Jackson's book and shows that Wilde's literary credentials almost a quarter of a century later are still being critically assessed. By the mid-1920s, with the dominance of literary modernism's preferences and aesthetics, Edward Shanks views Wilde's art as being generally derivative and made up of a succession of borrowings.

Nevertheless, Shanks sees in Wilde a character and personality that had come to represent a literary phase in English history, that of decadence. As a historian and a critic of literature, Shanks remarks at the conclusion of his essay on the role Wilde played as a fundamental part, if not as the symbol, of this artistic milieu. And yet Shanks's essay itself becomes something of a historical document, as much a summary of those critical tastes dominated by modernist perspectives as it is a snapshot of the attitudes of those involved in the early days of English literature as a discipline within British universities.

Ambrose Bierce "Prattle" (1882)

Ambrose Bierce was an American short story writer, journalist, and satirist. He was the editor of the weekly satirical magazine *The Wasp* from 1881 to 1885. The often savage comments he committed to print about various writers earned him the nickname of Bitter Bierce. But he was highly regarded as an author and known as much for the careful choice of wording and spare style in his own writing as for his scathing attacks on others.

The following extract is an example of the type of attack Wilde often suffered, but it is remarkable for its rigorous concentration and remorselessness. Wilde had garnered some success with the publication of a collection of poems in 1881 and parlayed that same success into a lecture tour of the United States. Bierce is responding to the interest and fanfare that greeted Oscar upon his arrival. Bierce lets no opportunity pass to denounce vehemently Wilde as a man, a speaker, and an artist. But Bierce's attack is not shallowly vindictive. Within the vituperative flood of condemnation, he addresses several important issues: the question of whether Wilde had proved himself sufficiently in the literary domain to match the praise that had been heaped on him, the validity of Wilde's claim to be leading a renaissance in the arts, and the responsibility the adoring public of London held for Wilde's taking to heart his own spectacular press.

The use of American slang is not uncommon in Bierce's work; he wrote as much for the man on the street as he did for literary elites. Its use highlights the important tension between Bierce's down-to-earth no-nonsense bluntness and his attitude about London's love affair with Wilde. It displays a sentiment not uncommon in critical appraisals at the time in the United States. To many American reviewers, Wilde's witticisms were seen as insubstantial, as simply clever rather than witty, and his aesthetic views as disposable fripperies. In large part, Wilde was perceived on his tour as a faddish object of amusement, rather than as an artist of any serious caliber or temperament. If Bierce's views are unusual in the severity of their delivery, the underlying sentiment was nevertheless seen on both sides of the Atlantic and is still apparent in some criticism today.

That sovereign of insufferables, Oscar Wilde, has ensued with his opulence of twaddle and his penury of sense. He has mounted his hind legs and blown crass vapidities through the bowel of his neck, to the capital edification of circumjacent fools and foolesses, fooling with their foolers. He has tossed off the top of his head and uttered himself in copious overflows of ghastly bosh. The ineffable dunce has nothing to say and says it—says it with a liberal embellishment of bad delivery, embroidering it with reasonless vulgarities of attitude, gesture and attire. There was never an impostor so hateful, a blockhead so stupid, a crank so variously and offensively daft. Therefore is the she fool enamored of the feel of his tongue in her ear to tickle her understanding.

The limpid and spiritless vacuity of this intellectual jellyfish is in ludicrous contrast with the rude but robust mental activities that he came to quicken and inspire. Not only has he no thoughts, but no thinker. His lecture is mere verbal ditch-water—meaningless, trite and without coherence. It lacks even the nastiness that exalts and refines his verse. Moreover, it is obviously his own; he had not even the energy and independence to steal it. And so, with a knowledge that would equip an idiot to dispute with a cast-iron dog, an eloquence to qualify him for the duties of caller on a hog-ranch and an imagination adequate to the conception of a tom-cat, when fired by contemplation of a fiddle-string, this consummate and star-like youth, missing everywhere his heaven-appointed functions and offices, wanders about, posing as a statue of himself, and, like the sun-smitten image of Memnon, emitting meaningless murmurs in the blaze of women's eyes. He makes me tired.

And this gawky gowk has the divine effrontery to link his name with those of Swinburne, Rossetti and Morris—this dunghill he-hen would fly with eagles. He dares to set his tongue to the honored name of Keats. He is the leader, quoth'a, of a *renaissance* in art, this man who cannot draw—of a revival in letters, this man who cannot write! This littlest and looniest of a brotherhood of simpletons, whom the wicked wits of London, haling him dazed from his obscurity, have crowned and crucified as King of the Cranks, has accepted the distinction in stupid good faith and our foolish people take him at his word. Mr. Wilde is pinnacled upon a dazzling eminence but the earth still trembles to the dull thunder of the kicks that set him up.

—Ambrose Bierce, "Prattle," *Wasp*, March 31, 1882

W.B. Yeats "Oscar Wilde's Last Book" (1891)

William Butler Yeats was an Irish poet, dramatist, and statesman and became one of the leading literary figures of the twentieth century. In 1891, Yeats was living in London and had only just embarked on his literary career. The year before, he had founded a group with a fellow poet, Ernest Rhys, called the Rhymer's Club that would go on to publish two anthologies of verse. Several members of the group were friends and associates of Wilde's, and the club's members, while promoting a variety of poetic styles and interests, were broadly considered to be followers of Wilde's aestheticism.

This extract is written by a young fellow countryman who is beginning his poetic career in the metropolis of London where Wilde is already the leading literary light. It is unsurprising that Yeats praises Wilde, but the younger man's appraisal of the older is subtle and insightful: He appreciates the "Irishness" of Wilde's wit and paradoxes, his teasing the English for their stubborn matter-of-factness and lack of humor. Yeats points out that there is no moral harm to Wilde's writing, that the attacks made on Wilde in the English press on grounds of immorality are ridiculous. Yeats also raises a question central to an understanding of Wilde and his art: the question of sincerity and veracity. Yeats understands that truth is based on one's own point of view, an insight to which Wilde's English critics are blinded by their own self-centeredness and their presumption that everyone else thinks as they do. Because John Bull—the nickname for the figure of the "solidly" virtuous Englishman—believes something is true does not make it so. Wilde, as Yeats remarks, is simply asking his readers to query critically all that they presume to be factual. It is the subtlety of Wilde's own critical mind that Yeats highlights at the conclusion of the extract as being of particular value.

We have the irresponsible Irishman in life, and would gladly get rid of him. We have him now in literature and in the things of the mind, and are compelled perforce to see that there is a good deal to be said for him. The men I described to you the other day under the heading, "A Reckless Century," thought they might drink, dice, and shoot each other to their hearts' content, if they did but do it gaily and gallantly, and here now is Mr. Oscar Wilde, who does not care what strange opinions he defends or what time-honoured virtue he makes laughter of, provided he does it cleverly. Many were injured by the escapades of the rakes and duellists, but no man is likely to be the worse for Mr. Wilde's shower of paradox. We are not likely to poison any one because he writes with appreciation of Wainwright—art critic and poisoner—nor have I heard that there has been any increased mortality among deans because the good young hero of his last book tries to blow up one with an infernal machine; but upon the other hand we are likely enough to gain something of brightness and refinement from the deft and witty pages in which he sets forth these matters.

"Beer, bible, and the seven deadly virtues have made England what she is," wrote Mr. Wilde once; and a part of the Nemesis that has fallen upon her is a complete inability to understand anything he says. *We* should not find him so unintelligible—for much about him is Irish of the Irish. I see in his life and works an extravagant Celtic crusade against Anglo-Saxon stupidity. "I labour under a perpetual fear of not being misunderstood," he wrote, a short time since, and from behind this barrier of misunderstanding he peppers John Bull with his pea-shooter of wit, content to know there are some few who laugh with him. There is scarcely an eminent man in London who has not one of those little peas sticking somewhere about him. "Providence and Mr. Walter Besant have exhausted the obvious," he wrote once, to the deep indignation of Mr. Walter Besant; and of a certain notorious and clever, but coldblooded Socialist, he said, "he has no enemies, but is intensely disliked by all his friends." Gradually people have begun to notice what a very great number of those little peas are lying about, and from this reckoning has sprung up a great respect for so deft a shooter, for John Bull, though he does not understand wit, respects everything that he can count up and number and prove to have bulk. He now sees beyond question that the witty sayings of this man whom he has so long despised are as plenty as the wood blocks in the pavement of Cheapside. As a last resource he has raised the cry that his tormentor is most insincere, and Mr. Wilde replies in various ways that it is quite an error to suppose that a thing is true because John Bull sincerely believes it. Upon the other hand, if he did not believe it, it might have some chance of being true. This controversy is carried on upon the part of John by the newspapers; therefore, those who only read them have as low an opinion of Mr. Wilde as those who read books have a high one. *Dorian Grey* with all its faults of method, is a wonderful book. *The Happy Prince* is a volume of as pretty fairy tales as our generation has seen; and *Intentions* hides within its immense paradox some of the most subtle literary criticism we are likely to see for many a long day.

—W.B. Yeats, "Oscar Wilde's Last Book,"
(1891), *Uncollected Prose*, ed. John P. Frayne,
1970, vol. 1, pp. 203–204

ARTHUR SYMONS "AN ARTIST IN ATTITUDES: OSCAR WILDE" (1901)

Arthur Symons was an English poet, critic, and journalist. He was an acquaintance of Wilde's, if not close enough to be called a friend, but he was associated with Wildean aestheticism for much of the 1890s. At the end of the decade he would publish a review full of praise for Wilde's poem "The Ballad of Reading Gaol" in the *Pall Mall Gazette*, an article with which Wilde was said to have been delighted. After the decline in the popularity of 1890s aestheticism, Symons was the foremost agent for critically importing the poetry and poetics of the French symbolists to England.

This extract is something of a requiem, for Wilde had died only a few months earlier. It begins by using "The Ballad" as a springboard to discuss Wilde's aesthetic attitudes. Symons remarks that there were those who believed that the poem could only have been written after Wilde's time in prison, that his confrontation with a harsh reality forced him, for the first time, to deal with the actual hardships of life when he had always before donned various postures and attitudes. But these readers were proved wrong, for, after the publication of "The Ballad," Wilde would publish nothing else. Symons explores the attitudinizing of Wilde, seeing in it the fundamental artistic character of the man. Symons's practiced, critical eye appraises the purpose and deliberation behind the attitudes Wilde had adopted until the end of his life.

The striking image used by Symons is that of Wilde as a juggler of souls. For Symons, these souls, or personalities, are real; his opinion of Wilde is that of a man to whom they were simply baubles to be revealed one by one, with no connection between what had gone before and what might come after. Symons suggests that these souls had lives of their own that went unrecognized by Wilde but that, on occasion, they would become "so real" that even Wilde was forced to accept their power to control his own, and his audience's, perceptions. But Symons appreciates Wilde's skill in juggling these personalities so well that the public never noticed his sleight of hand, even if the artist himself did. These various personas were a series of masks for Wilde, to be worn and disposed of when their aesthetic purpose was accomplished. Symons insightfully initiates the critical query, still being asked of Wilde today, about what lies behind the mask when it becomes the sole identity of its wearer?

Symons sees Wilde as neither sage, poet, nor artist but as a dramatic intellect temporarily adopting the attitudes of each. Wilde's fundamental motivation was his insistence on divorcing art and life into two utterly separate spheres. It allowed him to adopt his attitudes and masks, to juggle the souls for his admiring audience. Symons is of the opinion that there have been those who have praised Wilde's art either too much or not enough; he believes that Wilde should be judged not as a literary artist but as his period's "supreme artist in intellectual attitudes." This perception, suggested only a few months after Wilde's death, continues to strongly influence critical approaches to Wilde's art and ideas today.

—◦//◦—   —◦//◦—   —◦//◦—

When the *Ballad of Reading Gaol* was published, it seemed to some people that such a return to, or so startling a first acquaintance with, real things, was precisely what was most required to bring into relation, both with life and art, an extraordinary talent, so little in relation with matters of common experience, so fantastically alone in a region of intellectual abstractions. In this poem, where a style formed on other lines seems startled at finding itself used for such new purposes, we see a great spectacular intellect, to which, at last, pity and terror have come in their own person, and no longer as puppets in a play. In its sight, human life has always been something acted on the stage; a comedy in which it is the wise man's part to sit aside and laugh, but in which he may also disdainfully take part, as in a carnival, under any mask. The unbiassed, scornful intellect, to which humanity has never been a burden, comes now to be unable to sit aside and laugh, and it has worn and looked behind so many masks that there is nothing left desirable in illusion. Having seen, as the artist sees, further than morality, but with so partial an eyesight as to have overlooked it on the way, it has come at length to discover morality in the only way left possible, for itself. And, like most of those who, having "thought themselves weary," have made the adventure of putting thought into action, it has had to discover it sorrowfully, at its own incalculable expense. And now, having become so newly acquainted with what is pitiful, and what seems most unjust, in the arrangement of human affairs, it has gone, not unnaturally, to an extreme, and taken, on the one hand, humanitarianism, on the other realism, at more than their just valuation, in matters of art. It is that odd instinct of the intellect, the necessity of carrying things to their furthest point of development, to be more logical than either life or art, two very wayward and illogical things, in which conclusions do not always follow from premises.

Well, and nothing followed, after this turning-point, as it seemed, in a career. "Whatever actually occurs is spoiled for art," Oscar Wilde has said. One hoped, but he had known at least himself, from the beginning. Nothing followed. Wit remained, to the very end, the least personal form of speech, and thus the kindest refuge for one who had never loved facts in themselves. "I am dying beyond my means" was the last word of his which was repeated to me.

His intellect was dramatic, and the whole man was not so much a personality as an attitude. Without being a sage, he maintained the attitude of a sage; without being a poet, he maintained the attitude of a poet; without being an artist, he maintained the attitude of an artist. And it was precisely in his attitudes that he was most sincere. They represented his intentions; they stood for the better, unrealised part of himself. Thus his attitude, towards life and towards art, was untouched by his conduct; his perfectly just and essentially dignified assertion of the artist's place in the world of thought and the place of beauty in the material world being in nowise invalidated by his own failure to create pure beauty or to become a quite honest artist. A talent so vividly at work as to be almost genius was incessantly urging him into action, mental action. Just as the appropriate word always came to his lips, so the appropriate attitude always found him ready to step into it, as into his own shadow. His mind was eminently reasonable, and if you look closely into his wit, you will find that it has always a basis of logic, though it may indeed most probably be supported by its apex at the instant in which he presents it to you. Of the purely poetical quality he had almost nothing; his style, even in prose, becomes insincere, a bewildering echo of Pater or of some French writer, whenever he tries to write beautifully. Such imagination as he had was like the flickering of light along an electric wire, struck by friction out of something direct and hard, and, after all, only on the surface.

"But then it is only the Philistine," he has said, in his essay on Wainewright, "who seeks to estimate a personality by the vulgar test of production. This young dandy sought to be somebody rather than to do something. He recognised that Life itself is an art, and has its modes of style no less than the arts that seek to express it." "Art never expresses anything but itself," he has said, in another essay in the same book, so aptly called *Intentions*; and that "principle of his new aesthetics" does but complete his view of the function of life. Art and life are to be two things, absolutely apart, each a thing made to a pattern, not a natural, or, as he would take it to be, an accidental, growth. It is the old principle of art for art's sake, pushed to its furthest limits, where every truth sways over into falsehood. He tells us that "the highest art rejects the burden of the human spirit, and gains more from a new medium or a fresh material than she does from any enthusiasm for art, or from any lofty passion, or from any fresh awakening of the human consciousness." But he forgets that he is only discussing technique, and that faultless technique, though art cannot exist without it, is not art.

And so with regard to life. Realising as he did that it is possible to be very watchfully cognisant of the "quality of our moments as they pass," and to shape them after one's own ideal much more continuously and consciously than most people have ever thought of trying to do, he made for himself many souls, souls of intricate pattern and elaborate colour, webbed into infinite tiny cells, each the home of a strange perfume, perhaps a poison. Every soul had its own secret, and was secluded from the soul which had gone before it or was to come after it. And this showman of souls was not always aware that he was juggling with real things, for to him they were no more than the coloured glass balls which the juggler keeps in the air, catching them one after another. For the most part the souls were content to be playthings; now and again they took a malicious revenge, and became so real that even the juggler was aware of it. But when they became too real he had to go on throwing them into the air and catching them, even though the skill of the game had lost its interest for him. But as he never lost his self-possession, his audience, the world, did not see the difference.

Among these souls there was one after the fashion of Flaubert, another after the fashion of Pater, others that had known Baudelaire, and Huysmans, and De Quincey, and Swinburne. Each was taken up, used, and dropped, as in a kind of persistent illustration of "the truth of masks." "A truth in art is that whose contradictory is also true." Well, it was with no sense of contradiction that the critic of beautiful things found himself appealing frankly to the public in a series of the wittiest plays that have been seen on the modern stage. It was another attitude, that was all; something external, done for its own sake, "expressing nothing but itself," and expressing, as it happened by accident, precisely what he himself was best able to express.

It may be, perhaps, now that the man is dead, that those who admired him too much or too little will do him a little justice. He was himself systematically unjust, and was never anxious to be understood too precisely, or to be weighed in very level balances. But he will be remembered, if not as an artist in English literature, at all events in the traditions of our time, as the supreme artist in intellectual attitudes.

—Arthur Symons, "An Artist in Attitudes:
Oscar Wilde," (1901), *Studies in Prose and Verse,*
1904, pp. 124–128

MAX BEERBOHM "A LORD OF LANGUAGE" (1905)

Max Beerbohm was an English novelist, short story writer, essayist, journalist, parodist, and caricaturist. He was associated with Wilde's aestheticism while still a student at Oxford, and, when he arrived on the literary scene in London after completing his studies, he was an immediate success as the youngest wit in the metropolis. He knew Wilde but was careful to keep a certain distance from him; whether this was because he feared his own writing would be cast in Wilde's shadow or for personal reasons is unknown. He was, however, broadly sympathetic when Wilde was imprisoned as the following extract shows; but that sympathy, as is typical of Beerbohm's writing, is often framed by his uniquely sardonic humor.

Beerbohm addresses those critics who viewed *De Profundis*, Wilde's posthumously published, although at this point still abbreviated, letter to Lord Alfred Douglas from prison, as a transformation of his art. Two basic misunderstandings emerge in this assessment in Beerbohm's mind: first, that Wilde was primarily a wit, and second, that the letter was an example of a sincere, humbled attitude on the part of the artist. Beerbohm addresses both points, stating that Wilde's wit was not his primary artistic ability, that his witticisms sprang from a profound capacity for thought and from a philosophical intellect. He then contends that the seriousness of Wilde's thoughts was balanced by his playful adoption of roles, and Beerbohm sees in the emotion and humility on display in *De Profundis* simply another mask assumed by the artist.

Beerbohm reserves his praise for Wilde's manner of expression rather than the meaning of his prose, and he sees the manner of expression in *De Profundis* as unchanged from Wilde's earlier work. Wilde is described as "immutable" in his character, unchangeable even after his ordeal in prison. This "immutability" might seem to be at odds with everything else that Beerbohm and other critics have suggested concerning Wilde's adoption of a succession of attitudes; it is not. What Beerbohm intends is to suggest that Wilde's attitudinizing remained constant throughout and after his incarceration. *De Profundis* is, for Beerbohm, an example of this unchanged manner, an artistic pose adopted by Wilde.

There was a coincidence last week in London. An exhibition of Whistler's paintings was opened, and a book by Oscar Wilde was published; and all the critics are writing, and the gossips gossiping, very glibly, about the greatness of Whistler, and about the greatness of Oscar Wilde. Whistler during the 'seventies and 'eighties, and Oscar Wilde during the 'eighties and early 'nineties, cut very prominent figures in London; and both were by the critics and the gossips regarded merely as clever *farceurs*. Both, apart from their prominence, were doing serious work; but neither was taken at all seriously. Neither was thanked. Whistler got a farthing damages, Oscar Wilde two years' hard labour. None of the critics or gossips took exception to either verdict. Time has rolled on. Both men are dead. A subtly apocalyptic thing, for critics and gossips (especially in England), is the tomb; and praises are by envious humanity sung the more easily when there is no chance that they will gratify the subjects of them. And so, very glibly, very blandly, we are all magnifying the two men whom we so lately belittled. M. Rodin was brought over to open the Whistler exhibition. Perhaps the nation will now commission him to do a statue of Oscar Wilde. *Il ne manque que ça.*

Some of the critics, wishing to reconcile present enthusiasm with past indifference, or with past obloquy, have been suggesting that *De Profundis* is quite unlike any previous work of Oscar Wilde—a quite sudden and unrelated phenomenon. Oscar Wilde, according to them, was gloriously transformed by incarceration. Their theory comprises two fallacies. The first fallacy is that Oscar Wilde had been mainly remarkable for his wit. In point of fact, wit was the least important of his gifts. Primarily, he was a poet, with a life-long passion for beauty; and a philosopher, with a life-long passion for thought. His wit, and his humour (which was of an even finer quality than his wit), sprang from a very solid basis of seriousness, as all good wit or humour must. They were not essential to his genius; and, had they happened not to have been there at all, possibly his genius would, even while he himself was flourishing, have been recognised in England, where wisdom's passport is dulness, and gaiety of manner damns. The right way of depreciating Oscar Wilde would have been to say that, beautiful and profound though his ideas were, he never was a real person in contact with realities. He created his poetry, created his philosophy: neither sprang from his own soul, or from his own experience. His ideas were for the sake of ideas, his emotions for the sake of emotions. This, I take it, is just what Mr. Robert Ross means, when, in his admirable introduction to *De Profundis,* he speaks of Oscar Wilde as a man of "highly intellectual and artificial nature." Herein, too, I find the key to an old mystery; why Oscar Wilde, so saliently original a man, was so much influenced by the work of other writers; and why he, who none was more fertile in invention, did sometimes stoop to plagiarism. If an idea was beautiful or profound, he cared not what it was, nor whether it was his or another's. In *De Profundis* was he, at length, expressing something that he really and truly felt? Is the book indeed a heart-cry? It is pronounced so by the aforesaid critics. There we have the second fallacy.

I think no discerning reader can but regard the book as essentially the artistic essay of an artist. Nothing seemed more likely than that Oscar Wilde, smitten down from his rosy-clouded pinnacle, and dragged through the mire, and cast among the flints, would be *diablement change en route*. Yet lo! he was unchanged. He was still precisely himself. He was still playing with ideas, playing with emotions. "There is only one thing left for me now," he writes, "absolute humility." And about humility he writes many beautiful and true things. And, doubtless, while he wrote them, he had the sensation of humility. Humble he was not. Emotion was not seeking outlet: emotion came through its own expression. The artist spoke, and the man obeyed. The attitude was struck, and the heart pulsated to it. Perhaps a Cardinal Archbishop, when he kneels to wash the feet of the beggars, is filled with humility, and revels in the experience. Such was Oscar Wilde's humility. It was the luxurious complement of pride. In *De Profundis,* for the most part, he is frankly proud—proud with the natural pride of a man so richly endowed as he, and arrogant with all his old peculiar arrogance. Even "from the depths" he condescended. Nor merely to mankind was he condescending. He enjoyed the greater luxury of condescending to himself. Sometimes the condescension was from his present self to his old self; sometimes from his old self to his present self. Referring to the death of his mother, "I, once a lord of language," he says, "have no words in which to express my anguish and my shame." Straightway, he proceeds to revel in the survival of that lordship, and refutes in a fine passage his own dramatic plea of impotence. "She and my father had bequeathed to me a name they had made noble and honoured . . . I had disgraced that name eternally. I had made it a low byword among low people. I had dragged it through the very mire. I had given it to brutes that they might make it brutal, and to fools that they might turn it into folly. What I suffered then, and still suffer, is not for pen to write or paper to record." Yet pen wrote it, and paper recorded it, even so. And sorrow was turned to joy by the "lord of language."

"A lord of language." Certainly that was no idle boast. Fine as are the ideas and emotions in *De Profundis,* it is the actual writing—the mastery of prose—that most delights me. Except Ruskin in his prime, no modern writer has achieved through prose the limpid and lyrical effects that were achieved by Oscar Wilde. One does not seem to be reading a written thing. The words sing. There is nothing of that formality, that hard and cunning precision, which marks so much of the prose that we admire, and rightly admire. The meaning is artificial, but the expression is always magically natural and beautiful. The simple words seem to grow together like wild flowers. In his use of rhyme and metre, Oscar Wilde was academic—never at all decadent, by the way, as one critic has suggested. But the prose of *Intentions,* and of his plays, and of his fairy-stories, was perfect in its lively and unstudied grace. It is a joy to find in this last prose of his the old power, all unmarred by the physical and mental torments that he had suffered.

Oscar Wilde was immutable. The fineness of the book as a personal document is in the revelation of a character so strong that no force of circumstance could change it, or even modify it. In prison Oscar Wilde was still himself—still with the same artistry in words, still with the same detachment from life. We see him here as the spectator of his own tragedy. His tragedy was great. It is one of the tragedies that will live always in romantic history. And the protagonist had an artist's joy in it. Be sure that in the dock of the Old Bailey, in his cell at Reading, on "the centre platform of Clapham Junction," where he stood "in convict dress, and handcuffed, for the world to look at," even while he suffered he was consoled by the realisation of his sufferings and of the magnitude of his tragedy. Looking joyously forward to his release, "I hope," he says, "to be able to recreate my creative faculty." It is a grim loss to our literature that the creative faculty, which prison-life had not yet extinguished in him, did not long survive his liberation. But, broken as he was thereafter, and powerless, and aimless, the invincible artist in him must have had pleasure in contemplation of himself draining the last bitter dregs of the cup that Fate had thrust on him.

—Max Beerbohm, "A Lord of Language,"
Vanity Fair, March 2, 1905, p. 309

WILFRID M. LEADMAN "THE LITERARY POSITION OF OSCAR WILDE" (1906)

The Westminster Review was England's leading journal for radical thinkers. Here, the critic Wilfrid Leadman expresses his belief that Wilde's rehabilitation as an artist and thinker, which he sees as having begun in British social circles then advanced in the United States and on the Continent, will continue until his literary importance and genius are fully recognized.

Leadman states that the disgust in which Wilde was held existed even before his incarceration and was fundamentally caused by an English lack of aesthetic appreciation. Because Wilde's views ran counter to those generally held among the "stolid" and "Puritanical" public, their misunderstanding led to attacks both aesthetic and personal. Wilde's downfall was simply the culmination of more than a decade's worth of general cultural distaste. Leadman maintains that Wilde was a "kaleidoscope puzzle" even to his friends; the man was too complex an individual, his identities too multiform, to ever be fully understood.

Leadman appeals for an appreciation of Wilde's art divorced from his private life. He suggests that the publications of "The Ballad of Reading Gaol" and *De Profundis* have done much to address public concerns with Wilde's moral character and the ethical preoccupations of his art, and hopes that the amelioration of the public view of Wilde will lead to an appreciation of his earlier works. This critical position concerning the relationship between the life and art of Wilde is central to an understanding of each. Much criticism has concentrated on seeing Wilde's political and sexual life as codified in his work, or, as in Leadman's extract, is intent on an assessment of Wilde's art as being, to varying degrees, distinct from his life. Leadman suggests that for the general public to be placed in a position to fully appreciate Wilde's thought, his sexual orientation must be understood "scientifically" as a "pathology" and that this viewpoint will break down the most serious hurdle for the puritanical Englishman in admiring Wilde's literary work. Leadman maintains that Wilde's moral indiscretions should not stop an appreciation for the profundity of his thought, and, indeed, in several places in the following extract, he argues for the moral character of Wilde's own writing.

—✶✶✶✶— —✶✶✶✶— —✶✶✶✶—

Maeterlinck has shown us in one of his admirable essays how impossible and how absurd it is to attempt to reconcile human affairs with the idea of an intelligent external justice impartially and invariably meting out good for good and evil for evil. All injustice springs originally from man himself or from what we are pleased to call Nature. The intelligence of Nature is purely mechanical; she has smiles and frowns for both moral and immoral alike, without regard to character or conduct. The "justice" or "injustice" of man is purely arbitrary, hence its seeming inexplicability. In no sense, perhaps, is the cruelty and caprice of human justice shown more painfully than in the history of literature. Here and there, scattered over the globe, we find lonely and unrecognised geniuses whose messages have faded and remain forgotten because no one has been found to appreciate or to understand them. And too often the fault lay, not in the message or its deliverer, but in the world. On the other hand we find writers (not always so deserving) concerning whose high position the world has spoken decisively. She has placed them on lofty pedestals. And those whom she chooses for this honour are usually the writers who have made a successful appeal to some strong force in human nature. They count their followers by millions; for they have a straightforward message for plain minds. True, in distant years their names may fade for ever to make room for other names bearing similar messages, but, whatever their ultimate fate be, they have at least the satisfaction of present glory and the supreme consolation of being understood by their fellows. In the contemplation of these darlings of public opinion we feel no pain; but, when we turn to the victims of that same public opinion, we cannot but feel angered at the grotesque caprice of human justice. Among the writers so rejected by the world there are some whom she has spurned simply because she has not troubled to understand them. Prominent among this mournful group is Oscar Wilde. Around that hapless man controversy incessantly played in the past and apparently will continue to play in the future. His whole literary work (plays, poems, essays, and fiction) in vain cried out for just criticism—prejudice, misconception, and a strained sense of respectability refused it. His few admirers were dubbed a senseless clique dazzled by the showy glitter of his language. Wilde was always considered a mere "poseur." Fault was found with all his writings. It was said that his prose was disfigured by incongruous ornament; his poetry was a feeble echo of Keats and Swinburne. His wonderful essays—especially "The Decay of Lying" and "The Soul of Man"—were admired only for their peculiar brilliance; their inherent depths of philosophy was overlooked. His plays were deemed conventional in construction and overloaded with spurious wit. Great and undue stress was invariably laid on the man's eccentricities; in the public eye Wilde was only a witty fellow yearning for celebrity and capable of performing weird literary antics to attain that object. He is indeed a tragic figure. Laughed at in his youth, misunderstood in his maturity, spurned in his closing years, accused of plagiarism, blamed for his love of posture, constantly charged with artificiality, an object of unceasing attack from pulpit and press—in a word, roundly abused all his life—Wilde would seem to have small chance, in this country, at any rate, of literary fame. Long before the catastrophe of 1895 he had an extraordinary amount of prejudice against him. His downfall was the crowning condemnation. After that it looked as though he were indeed doomed to an eternal outer darkness. And yet, leaving the question of his conduct on one side, his sole fault was simply his unswerving fidelity to his own intellectual bias. He could not write about ordinary things in an ordinary way. He could not present the British public with its favourite dish of love and sport. He was incapable of moulding his maxims on traditional conceptions of virtue and vice. It was, perhaps, inevitable that the uneducated British public should turn its back on one who at almost every opportunity flaunted in its face the most unusual doctrines. For it must be confessed, Oscar Wilde enunciated doctrines utterly alien to the ingrained Puritanism and athleticism of English people. The man who runs counter to national traditions and prejudices is bound to provoke bitter hostility. The man who, in this country, places art before muscle or sets the individual will above the conventional law, seems sure sooner or later to come to grief. Yet, in spite of his unpopularity, Wilde was never discouraged. Borne up by his own motto, "To be great is to be misunderstood," he moved steadily forward, and made his mark. True his influence was limited to the very few, but it existed and will expand further in the time to come. The unconventional will always thank him for his unflinching advocacy of things unconventional. The artist will remember him because he was one of the courageous few who helped to remove English theories of art from the tyranny of rigid tradition to the freedom of unfettered originality. He may have been rash, he may have been inclined to pose, his writings may show traces of plagiarism—an innocent sort of plagiarism that is almost a transformation—but there was always a thoroughness about his work which certainly deserved fairer consideration. To the average English mind his doctrines could only suggest the bizarre and the unnatural; but that was because the English mind had not yet learnt to appreciate an oblique point of view. Not that Wilde's outlook was always unusual. On the contrary, some of his short stories—especially "The Happy Prince," "The Star-Child," and "The Model Millionaire"—though necessarily tinted with his peculiar colouring, would satisfy the most exacting moralist by their tone of "poetic justice." If Wilde occasionally trampled on cherished national convictions or sometimes thrust strangely-hued flowers amongst our soberer blossoms, it was not from love of opposition; it was rather because he had to drift whither his fantastic and exuberant intellect listed.

Wilde's descent into the abyss seemed at the time to be the death-blow to what little influence he had already gained. The hasty verdict of a rather superficial morality said then that his influence must have been essentially unhealthy. From that time to the publication of De Profundis it was even deemed a breach of manners to allude to Wilde in any way. However, that interesting posthumous book has been the cause of a partial change of the public attitude. We are once more allowed to discuss Wilde's book without hearing a shocked "hush," or being suspected of loose views on moral matters. Whatever one's opinion may be as to the genuineness of the repentance shown in De Profundis, one may at any rate be deeply thankful for what it has undoubtedly done toward the rehabilitation of its author. He is no longer under a ban. He may eventually receive a high place in English literature. After all, his admitted writings cannot fairly be deemed unhealthy. Those who see "an undercurrent of nasty suggestion" in some of his literary productions must surely be so obsessed by their knowledge of his unfortunate behaviour as to lose all power of disconnecting two absolutely independent things, namely, his art and his private life. The ludicrous charges of immorality brought against that book of painted words and lordly language, *Dorian Gray,* fall to the ground at once when it is known that the book was written solely for money. As Mr. Sherard says in his *Life of Oscar Wilde,* no author would risk the financial success of a book by filling it with immoral teachings. The marvel to me is that Wilde managed to produce such a transcendent work of art under the pressure of such a prosaic stimulus.

In the past, before his downfall, Wilde's works were only read carefully by a select few. Others, it is true, granted a certain momentary admiration to his prose, but it was the sort of admiration involuntarily and temporarily evoked by gorgeous fireworks rather than the lasting admiration felt for a permanent object of art. Now, if justice is to be done to any author's work the impersonal attitude is imperative. The intellectual reader must sink his personal predilections, he must not keep asking himself whether he agree with this or that sentiment expressed by an author. It is not very hard to do. There are minds which dislike stories packed with scenes of love, but such minds need not on that account be debarred from appreciating the almost faultless love-scenes in *Richard Feverel.* Of course, when the reader is by nature in perfect accord with the writer's sentiments, the enjoyment will be fuller and more satisfactory than when his appreciation be acquired, but in both cases the object of the writer's genius will have been attained. In the case of Wilde's works there is a real necessity for impartiality of standpoint, because only the few are by nature and inclination in tune with his work. The majority must learn to put themselves into tune. Two difficulties—broadly speaking—hamper anything like a general and intelligent recognition of Wilde's genius. The first is undoubtedly the moral obliquity or seeming moral obliquity revealed by the criminal trial of 1895. The second is the lack of effort or ability to understand Oscar Wilde's trend of thought. Would that the former might be for ever forgotten! After all, his writings are of vastly more importance to posterity than his private conduct. The stolid Englishman, however, finds it hard to differentiate between a man's private character and his books. Certain unfortunate impressions received in 1895 cloud his honest judgment in the matter of Wilde's position in literature. Now this is not the place to discuss the pathological aspect of Oscar Wilde's conduct, but I may be permitted to say that his restitution—to be permanent—must depend on a fuller knowledge of an obscure branch of morbid pathology.

This at present, for obvious reasons, is impossible. No doubt *De Profundis* with its confession of humility and its partial admission of error will impress many minds favourably, but the more matter of fact minds care little whether that book be entirely sincere or merely a huge pose intended to transform public opinion. What they do care about is a *locus standi* based on sound scientific grounds. Once such a basis be generally accepted, perhaps the worst obstacle to the recognition of Wilde will have been taken away. Let it be admitted that Wilde erred greatly; then charity reminds us that there is such a thing as forgiveness of sin. Let it be granted that pathological research will explain and even excuse much of his conduct; common-sense will then bid us banish our rigid prudery and consign once and for all to oblivion what really has absolutely nothing to do with our unchecked contemplation of a great artist.

The other obstacle to an unbiassed conception of this writer's productions is not so easily defined as that just discussed, for the latter sprang into existence at a definite time, whilst this one had existed ever since Wilde published his first book of poems. From the beginning Wilde's ideas were diametrically opposed to all our eminently respectable British traditions of art. The reading world failed to grasp his meaning. And that was mainly due to what one may call our national inability to understand a creed whose keynote was the worship of beauty. We are, above all, a stolid race, in no way over-attracted by beauty; we certainly love personal cleanliness and comfort, but it is a cleanliness derived from cold water rather than from warm, and a comfort obtained from blankets and brick rather than from silks and marble. We cannot see the use of any one's making a fuss of a beautiful thing simply because of its beauty. Such a proceeding savours to us of lunacy or idolatry. And when Wilde, in 1881, burst upon our sober minds with his first book of poems—saturated as it was with a lavish reckless admiration of beauty—we felt that here indeed was a strange apostle teaching a still stranger cult. Coming, as this book did, on the heels of Wilde's aesthetic campaign—after all, but as pardonable youthful extravagance, and, as, Mr. Sherard points out, completely cured by that American tour, which taught a needed practical lesson—there was, perhaps, some reason for its hostile reception. "Here is a man," said the critics, "who values all glittering evanescence of a coloured bubble above morality itself." This sweeping opinion represented the belief of many critics at that time, and, unfortunately for Wilde, later events seemed confirmatory. In one sense possibly Wilde did set beauty above morality, but it was above the conventional conception of morality—that is something arbitrary and too often uncharitable—not above goodness. In any case, one must not base one's conception of Wilde's attitude towards morality on anything which he has written. Some men do, indeed, project their own personalities into their books, in spite of Wilde's splendid dictum: "To reveal art and to conceal the artist is the true aim of art. The artist can express everything." But one may be confident that the author of *Dorian Gray* has been guilty of no such literary soul-dissecting. An intimate friend of his—a man, perhaps, more fitted to speak authoritatively on this subject than any other man living—told me that Wilde only revealed *one* aspect of his own character in his books, and that not the most attractive aspect.

Read in the clear light of intelligent criticism, the first book of poems teaches only one thing, namely, that here is an author almost unique in his whole-hearted worship of form and colour, a worship, too, that is not casual, capricious, and superficial, but serious, terribly serious, and thoroughly healthy. Of course, all this was horribly unpractical, and most Englishmen, with their innate dislike of "hollow beauty," shrugged their shoulders. Wilde, in his first as in his later efforts, wrote only for minds attuned to his. Others must take the right attitude or else pass on elsewhere.

Wilde has plainly this to his credit that he never tried to win the public, never debased the art of literature by pandering to any popular movement. Of that exquisite set of allegories *The House of Pomegranates* he finely said (in answer to some mystified critics) that "it was intended neither for the British child nor for the British public." Indeed, some think that much, if not all, of his work was the accidental, irresponsible, yet irresistible overflow of an ever creative intellect, and not literature written with any definite purpose. On this question, however, it is better to keep an open mind.

Wilde had an inherent horror of the commonplace, and this seems to have led him occasionally into a rather strained effort after a rather petty kind of originality. Of course his numerous enemies laid hold of that habit and made it the foundation of a great deal of silly abuse. Frivolous, frothy remarks put into the mouths of some of Wilde's characters were solemnly quoted as part of Wilde's creed. Witty repartees deliberately torn from their proper context in his plays were seriously construed as Wilde's own gospel. The words of few men have undergone such distortion and misinterpretation as have those of this genius. One can only be thankful that now at any rate there are signs of the advent of Truth, there are signs of a strong fresh breeze sweeping away those murky mists and grotesque masks that have so long hidden the real Wilde. It is at last dawning on men's minds that his writings are not so much external ornament concealing a blank void, and that his wit is often wisdom, only occasionally nonsense. Some critics say that Wilde's art may be very entertaining and very clever, but that (with the exception of *De Profundis)* it leads us nowhere. But is that, even if true, a sound objection to his work? For some people, at any rate, it is refreshing to step aside from the hustle and bustle of literary missionaries and to enjoy a healthy rest with an author who does not burden his readers with any tedious lesson. As a matter of fact, whether Wilde had any fixed aim or not, his work most certainly points—and points clearly—to a definite goal. I think that there are those who will say that they have been led by this author to very fruitful regions. If some people feel that Wilde only takes them a giddy dance over tracts of glittering but useless beauty, there are others who feel that his restless flights helped them to realise the wonder of much that previously seemed common and graceless. What, pray, are many of Wilde's short stories, such as the "Young King" and "The Happy Prince," but artistically embroidered pleas for social reform? Who can read *Dorian Gray* intelligently without hearing the deep bass note of doom at first faint, but gradually growing louder and louder amid the brilliant cascade of frivolous treble notes till it drowns them in the final crash of just punishment for error? Can any one fail to note the stern moral lesson of *Salome?* Who can study his other plays carefully without learning the superb philosophy of human life that runs through them like a silver thread amid a many-hued skein? And who can help observing the high aspirations which lift so much of his verse out of the sphere of mere decorated rhyme? The truth is, Wilde's work bristles with moral advice, but—partly owing to his own oft-repeated condemnation of stories with a moral, and partly owing to the innate obtuseness of most of his readers—it is constantly overlooked.

In the early nineties Wilde's position was almost unique; he was looked upon as a literary phenomenon defying satisfactory solution. His art bewildered, amazed, repelled; if a few here hailed him as worthy to rank with intellectual giants, a multitude there said his art was unreal, frothy, and sometimes dangerous. He was a kaleidoscope puzzle even to his own friends. This is shown by the impressions of him recorded by various personal friends; they all seemed to see a different man: none of their presentations agree. Still, Wilde kept on his way gyrating giddily onward. His art must sooner or later bear fruit and find its home; such ability could not be destined to be wasted. Then, just as he seemed on the point of grasping honour and glory, there came in his career that fatal crisis, the one bright spot in which was, perhaps, that it saved him from worse things. Prison life steadied him. It helped him to take a fuller, broader view of life, to recognise how incomplete had been his former life when it confined itself to the enjoyment of this world's splendour and refused to acknowledge or share in the world's sorrow. In the quiet of his cell he could write the pleading, passionate prose afterwards given us as *De Profundis.* This book has struck the public imagination. And to me, of all the puzzling problems connected with the unfortunate Oscar Wilde, none is so inexplicable as this. A book, the keynote of which is an abject almost grovelling humility, has captivated the hearts of a people whose chief characteristics are sturdiness and independence of character. It may seem a dreadful statement, but if I were asked to name any book by Wilde that was not quite healthy in tone, I should promptly mention *De Profundis*. At the same time, I should hasten to add that the unhealthy part of the book was the unavoidable outcome of the author's terrible position. The crushed must needs be very humble.

But, apart from that one demoralising note of excessive humility, *De Profundis* is a splendid progression of noble thoughts leading in very truth from the dank gutter to the gleaming stars. The price paid for its evolution by the author was awful, but, as a writer said recently in the *Hibbert Journal*, it may have been absolutely necessary. Both this book and *A Ballad of Reading Gaol* fill the gaps left in Oscar Wilde's earlier work—gaps which might have remained empty but for his downfall. Neither of these books is, perhaps, any real advance (from a purely literary point of view) on his former work. But because they are both serious, both more in accordance with the tastes of the "man in the street," they have effected a considerable change in the public attitude. It would be safe to say that Wilde's literary position was never less insecure than at the present time. The favourable reception awarded to his last two books has opened the door to a more sensible and fairer examination of all his books. And that is all we admirers of Wilde's genius demand. The rest—the eventual granting to Wilde of a niche in the temple of English literature—will follow in due course. Some of his work already smacks of "the day before yesterday," it is true; but much of it is imperishable, capable of standing the test of ages. Much of it represents some of the finest prose-poetry in our language. Oscar Wilde was our *one* English artist in words. At length a turning-point has been reached. Oscar Wilde is once more on trial, but it is a trial whose result can involve no disgrace, but which may—surely will—bring him a radiant wreath of fame. It will last long, for there is a strong array of witnesses on either side, and there is much up-hill work for his advocates. The scarlet flame of his disgrace still throws a lurid light on all his literary works, but it has begun to grow paler and smaller, and ere long it may become extinct, and in its place will dazzle forth the jewelled light of his undying intellect, teaching our descendants about the eternity of beauty and joy, but bidding them never forget the temporary reign of pain and sorrow, beseeching them to sweep away the tainted refuse that hides the crystal purity below, asking them for justice. And will not these requests be granted? On the Continent, in America, the great awakening has begun; there, the genius has triumphed over the convict, the sinner has been lost in the artist. Must it be said, then, by a later generation that Britain alone never forgave the strange errors of one of her brightest thinkers, but was content to let foreign hands raise him and his from the mire? Surely no; surely we are not so rich in intellectual wealth that we can afford to pass *any* of our artists by "on the other side."

Anyhow, when the haze of Time has finally covered all trace of the human frailties of Oscar Wilde, his genius, now slowly forcing its way upward through many a clogging obstacle, will rise resplendent and glorious before the eyes of an understanding posterity.

—Wilfrid M. Leadman, "The Literary Position
of Oscar Wilde," *Westminster Review*,
August 1906, pp. 201–208

J. Comyns Carr (1908)

J. Comyns Carr was an English art and drama critic, author, playwright, gallery director, and theater manager. He was an acquaintance of Wilde's as a member of the London literary, artistic, and theater scenes. In this brief extract, Comyns Carr admires the unique nature of Wilde's dramatic work, which he considers his best. He suggests that the art of prose and the art of drama are incomparable by nature and cannot borrow stylistically from each other. He praises Wilde for his understanding of this fact, for his avoidance of the pitfalls that the novelist may stumble on in his attempts to write for the theater. It may be that Comyns Carr is considering the attempt made by Henry James—one of the most famous novelists of the late nineteenth and early twentieth centuries—who was generally considered, by himself much less the public, to have been humiliated in his attempt at a costume drama, *Guy Domville* (a play that ran in the West End of London at the same time as Wilde's incredibly successful *An Ideal Husband* and *The Importance of Being Earnest*). Comyns Carr believes it was Wilde's ability to interpret the "serious situations in life" within the framework of drama that granted him such success. It remains a constant in critical assessments of Wilde that his dramatic touch, his sense of performance, and his ease in considered role-playing are examples of his genuine artistic abilities.

Wilde's best work was unquestionably, I think, done for the stage, and here it may be conceded he struck out a path of his own. He had the sense of the theatre, a genuine instinct for those moments in the conflict of character to which the proper resources of the theatre can grant both added force and

added refinement. It is not an uncommon assumption, especially among
writers of fiction, that the drama by comparison is an art of coarse fibre,
incapable, by reason of its limitations, of presenting the more intimate
realities of character, or the more delicate shades of feeling. The truth is that
each art has its own force, its own refinement, and cannot borrow them of
another. What is perfectly achieved in one form remains incomparable, and
for that very reason cannot in its completed form be appropriated by an art
that has other triumphs and is subject to other laws and conditions. And it is
here that the novelist so often breaks down in attempting to employ his own
special methods in the service of the stage. Wilde made no such blunder. By
constant study as well as by natural gift he knew well the arena in which he
was working when he chose the vehicle of the drama. His wit has perhaps been
over-praised; his epigrams so loudly acclaimed at the time bear the taint of
modishness that seems to render them already old-fashioned. But his grip of
the more serious situations in life, and his ability to exhibit and interpret them
by means genuinely inherent in the resources at the disposal of the dramatist,
are left beyond dispute.

—J. Comyns Carr, *Some Victorian Poets*,
1908, pp. 213–214

ST. JOHN HANKIN "THE COLLECTED PLAYS OF OSCAR WILDE" (1908)

St. John Hankin was an English playwright and journalist, involved along
with George Bernard Shaw and John Galsworthy in the promotion of the
"New Drama" of the Edwardian period. The formal importance of drama
to these critics and playwrights necessarily colors Hankin's reading of
Wilde in this extract from the *Fortnightly Review*. He considers Wilde
as actually despising the theatrical world, even though he had the gift
of being a "born dramatist." Unlike the playwright Henrik Ibsen, whom
Hankin describes as writing because he was attracted to the formal structure of drama, or Bernard Shaw, who wrote to influence society, Wilde is
here described as writing for the stage simply for financial reasons.

   Hankin does not attack Wilde for writing for money, but he believes
Wilde's was a dramatic talent wasted, both by the attitude taken by Wilde
himself and by the late nineteenth century's incapacity to make use of
and develop its finest talents. Wilde's *Salomé* is considered by Hankin to
be the author's greatest dramatic work but is presented as such because
Wilde wrote it with no intention of it ever being performed on the stage

and because he believed that his ideas were most readily presentable in dramatic form. In a short exploration of the textual history of *The Importance of Being Earnest*, Hankin remarks on its being cut down from four to three acts by Wilde for performance rather than for stylistic or aesthetic reasons, taking this as an example of Wilde's lack of care for the theater generally. That such an "amazingly brilliant . . . joke" could be hacked apart for reasons that had nothing to do with art seems Hankin's chief concern. Throughout this extract, it is the formal integrity of drama, and that of the author, that is maintained as being of major importance.

—✥— —✥— —✥—

The fact is, Wilde despised the theatre. He was a born dramatist in the sense that he was naturally equipped with certain very valuable gifts for writing for the stage. But he was not a dramatist from conviction in the sense that Ibsen was or that Mr. Shaw is. Ibsen wrote plays, not because play-writing seemed a particularly promising or remunerative calling in the Norway of his day. It did not. He wrote plays because the dramatic form irresistibly attracted him. Mr. Shaw writes plays because he believes in the stage as an influence, as the most powerful and the most far-reaching of pulpits. Wilde's attitude towards the theatre was utterly different from either of these. He wrote plays frankly for the market and because play-writing was lucrative. Of course, he put a certain amount of himself into them. No artist can help doing that. But no artist of Wilde's power and originality ever did it less. His plays were frankly manufactured to meet a demand and to earn money. There is, of course, no reason why an artist should not work for money. Indeed, all artists do so more or less. They have to live like their neighbours. Unhappily, Wilde wanted a great deal of money, and he wanted it quickly. He loved luxury, and luxury cannot be had for nothing. And if an artist wants a large income and wants it at once, he generally has to condescend a good deal to get it. Wilde condescended. He looked around him at the kind of stuff which other playwrights were making money by, examined it with contemptuous acumen, saw how it was done—and went and did likewise. The only one of his plays which seems to me to be written with conviction, because he had something to express and because the dramatic form seemed to him the right one in which to express it, is *Salomé*— and *Salomé* was not written for the theatre. When Wilde wrote it he had no idea of its ever being acted. But when Madame Bernhardt one day asked him in jest why he had never written her a play, he replied, equally in jest, "I have," and sent her *Salomé*. She read it, and, as we know, would have produced it in London if the Censor of Plays had not intervened. But when Wilde wrote it, it was not with a view to its ever being performed, and so his genius had free scope. He was writing to please himself, not to please a manager, and the result is that *Salomé* is his best play. *The Importance of Being Earnest* is written with conviction, in a sense. That is to say, it is the expression of the author's own temperament and his attitude towards life, not an insincere restatement of conventional theatrical ideas. But *The Importance of Being Earnest* is only a joke, though an amazingly brilliant one, and Wilde seems to have looked upon it with the same amused contempt with which he looked on its predecessors. Perhaps he did not realise how good it was. At least he treated it with scant respect, for the original script was in four acts, and these were boiled down into three and the loose ends joined up in perfunctory fashion for purposes of representation. I wonder whether there is any copy of that four-act version still in existence, by the way? It is just possible that a copy is to be found at the Lord Chamberlain's office, for it may have been submitted for license in its original form. If so, I hope Mr. Ross will obtain permission to copy it with a view to its publication. If the deleted act is half as delightful as the three that survive, every playgoer will long to read it. But that a man of Wilde's theatrical skill and experience should have written a play which required this drastic "cutting"—or should have allowed it to be so cut if it did not require it—is an eloquent proof of his contempt for play-writing as an art.

Yes, Wilde despised the drama, and the drama avenged itself. With his gifts for dialogue and characterisation, his very remarkable "sense of the theatre," he might have been a great dramatist if he had been willing to take his art seriously. But he was not willing. The result was that in the age of Ibsen and of Hauptmann, of Strindberg and Brieux, he was content to construct like Sardou and think like Dumas *fils*. Had there been a National Theatre in this country in his day, or any theatre of dignity and influence to which a dramatist might look to produce plays for their artistic value, not solely for their value to the box office, Wilde might, I believe, have done really fine work for it. But there was not. And Wilde loved glitter and success. It would not have amused him to write "uncommercial" masterpieces to be produced for half a dozen *matinees* at a Boxers' Hall. His ambition—if he can be said to have had any "ambition" at all where the theatre was concerned—did not lie in that direction. So he took the stage as he found it, and wrote "pot-boilers." It is not the least of the crimes of the English theatre of the end of the nineteenth century that it could find nothing to do with a fine talent such as Wilde's save to degrade and waste it.

—St. John Hankin, "The Collected Plays of Oscar Wilde,"
Fortnightly Review, May 1908, pp. 801–802

Lord Alfred Douglas
"The Genius of Oscar Wilde" (1908)

Alfred Douglas, poet and author, is still remembered today primarily as the lover of Wilde and because his father, Lord Queensberry, was instrumental in Wilde's downfall. The following extract was written in 1908, several years after Douglas had married the poet Olive Eleanor Custance and only a few years before he converted to Catholicism. Douglas had always had the reputation of being quick to anger and unforgiving of supposed slights. The following extract sees him taking the opportunity, on the publication of Wilde's *Complete Works*, to attack those critics, notably W.E. Henley, who had in their turn lambasted Wilde years before. The extract can be difficult reading, for Douglas seems immune, as his reputation had always suggested, to recognizing the vindictiveness and irony inherent to his own assaults on others.

There are two instances in the following extract that suggest Douglas's character. First, the scathing statements he makes about the deceased Henley, who is ironically accused by Douglas of berating those unable to defend themselves (the deceased Robert Louis Stevenson and the essentially destitute Wilde upon his release from prison). Secondly, Douglas distances himself from Wilde's homosexual conduct, stating that Wilde had indeed lived a "morally delinquent" life, but his works retained a moral dimension simply underlined his genius. Stunningly, Douglas would later claim that he had had no sexual relationship with Wilde and would threaten lawsuits against those who stated anything to the contrary. In this extract, he attacks those "Iscariots" who had, in their turn, betrayed Wilde, and Douglas does so with no sense of irony whatsoever.

Even considering this extract a fairly unmeasured eulogy to Wilde's ability, the very fact that Douglas can print such a piece reveals the point at which Wilde's reputation rehabilitation in the eyes of English society and the world of English letters had arrived. Douglas, remembering the journalistic attacks frequently endured by Wilde before and after his arrest, appreciates the stark contrast of contemporary praise for Wilde's work with the offensive reviews of the 1880s and 1890s. Often, he mockingly claims, the same journalists were responsible for both.

The publication in twelve volumes by Messrs. Methuen of the complete works of Oscar Wilde marks, in a striking way, the complete literary rehabilitation which this author has achieved. When one considers that at the time of

Oscar Wilde's downfall the whole of his copyrights could have been purchased for about £100, one cannot help entertaining grave suspicions as to the value of criticism in England. It must be remembered that the contempt with which Mr. Wilde's work was greeted by the general mass of contemporary criticism was not confined to the period after his condemnation. A reference to the files of the newspapers containing the criticisms of his plays as they came out would reveal the fact that almost without any exception they were received with mockery, ridicule, and rudeness.

It is intensely amusing to read the comments in the daily papers at the present juncture on the same subject. Oscar Wilde is referred to, as a matter of course, as a great genius and a great wit, and takes his place, in the eyes of those who write these articles, if not with Shakespeare, at any rate with the other highest exponents of English dramatic art. This, of course, is as it should be, but we wonder what the gentlemen who write these glowing accounts of Mr. Wilde's genius were doing at the time when these works of genius were being poured out, and why it should have been necessary for him in order to obtain recognition to undergo the processes of disgrace and death. With the exception of the *Ballad of Reading Gaol* and *De Profundis* every work of Oscar Wilde's was written before his downfall. If these works are brilliant works of genius now, they were so before, and the failure of contemporary criticism to appreciate this fact is a lasting slur upon the intelligence of the country.

If any one wishes to see a fair sample of the sort of criticism that used to be meted out to Oscar Wilde, let him turn to the dramatic criticism in *Truth* which appeared on the production of *Lady Windermere's Fan.* The article was, we believe, written by the late unlamented Clement Scott, and at this time of day, of course, Clement Scott's dramatic criticism is not taken seriously; but at the time it was taken quite seriously, and it is astounding to think that such a criticism should have passed absolutely unresented by anybody of importance, with the obvious exception of Oscar Wilde himself. Nowadays if a critic were to write such an article about a playwright of anything approaching the status of Oscar Wilde he would be refused admission to every theatre in London.

This state of affairs must give pause to those good people who have decided that the late W. E. Henley was a "great editor" and a "great critic." If Henley had been anything approaching either of these two things he would have seen and appreciated the value of Oscar Wilde; and if we refer to any of the much-lauded and much-regretted reviews or journals which were conducted by Henley, we find that so far from appreciating Oscar Wilde it was he who led the attack against him, an attack which was conducted with the utmost malevolence and violence, and which was, moreover, distinguished by a brainlessness which is almost incredible in a man who, like Henley (overrated as he is), was not without great talents of his own. That Henley was a great poet or a great writer of prose we have never believed, and the recent publication of his collected works by Messrs. Nutt does not give us any reason to alter our opinion.

The subject of the first great attack made by Henley on Oscar Wilde was *The Picture of Dorian Gray*. Henley affected to think this was an immoral work, and denounced it as such. Now, anybody who having read *Dorian Gray* can honestly maintain that it is not one of the greatest moral books ever written, is an ass. It is, briefly, the story of a man who destroys his own conscience. The visible symbol of that conscience takes the form of a picture, the presentment of perfect youth and perfect beauty, which bears on its changing surface the burden of the sins of its prototype. It is one of the greatest and most terrible moral lessons that an unworthy world has had the privilege of receiving at the hands of a great writer.

It is characteristic of what we may call the "Henleyean School" of criticism to confuse the life of a man with his art. It would be idle to deny that Oscar Wilde was an immoral man (as idle as it would be to contend that Henley was a moral one); but it is a remarkable thing that while Oscar Wilde's life was immoral his art was always moral. At the time when the attack by Henley was made there was a confused idea going about London that Oscar Wilde was a wicked man, and this was quite enough for Henley and the group of second-rate intelligences which clustered round him to jump to the conclusion that anything he wrote must also necessarily be wicked.

The crowning meanness of which Henley was guilty with regard to Oscar Wilde was his signed review of the *Ballad of Reading Gaol*. Henley was always an envious man; his attack on the memory of Stevenson is sufficient to show that; but he certainly surpassed himself when he wrote that disgraceful article. Surely a man possessing the smallest nobility of soul would have refrained at that juncture from attacking an old enemy—if, indeed, Wilde could properly be called an enemy of Henley's. Henley chose to make an unprovoked attack upon Wilde, from whom, as a matter of fact, he had received many benefits and kindnesses, but Wilde never retaliated in an ungenerous way, although his enormous intellectual superiority would have rendered it an easy task for him to pulverise Henley. It was always Wilde's way to take adverse criticism contemptuously, and, to the last, he never spoke of Henley with anything but good humour, albeit with some deserved disdain. The slow revenge of time has in this particular case bestirred itself to some purpose, and if we cannot say with justice "Who now reads Henley?" we can at any rate state very positively that for every reader that he has, Oscar Wilde has twenty. The reason is not far to seek. Wilde, putting aside his moral delinquencies, which have as much and as little to do with his works as the colour of his hair, was a great artist, a man who passionately loved his art. He was so great an artist that, in spite of himself, he was always on the side of the angels. We believe that the greatest art is always on the side of the angels, to doubt it would be to doubt the existence of God, and all the Henleys and all the Bernard Shaws that the world could produce would not make us change our opinion. It was all very well for Wilde to play with life, as he did exquisitely, and to preach the philosophy of pleasure, and plucking the passing hour; but the moment he sat down to write he became different. He saw things as they really were; he knew the falsity and the deadliness of his own creed; he knew that "the end of these things is Death;" and he wrote in his own inimitable way the words of Wisdom and Life. Like all great men, he had his disciples, and a great many of them (more than a fair share) turned out to be Iscariots; but it is his glory that he founded no school, no silly gang of catchword repeaters; he created no "journalistic tradition," and he was not referred to by ridiculous bumpkins occupying subordinate positions in the offices of third-rate Jewish publishing-houses as "dear old Wilde." Those who knew and loved him as a man and as a writer were men who had their own individualities and were neither his shadows nor his imitators. If they achieved any greatness they did it because they had greatness in them, and not because they aped "the master." Henley has his school of "Henley's young men," of whom we do not hear much nowadays. Wilde has his school of young men in those who copy what was least admirable in him, but from a literary point of view he has no school. He stands alone, a phenomenon in literature. From the purely literary point of view he was unquestionably the greatest figure of the nineteenth century. We unhesitatingly say that his influence on the literature of Europe has been greater than that of any man since Byron died, and, unlike Byron's, it has been all for good. The evil that he did, inasmuch as he did a tithe of the things imputed to him, was interred with his bones, the good (how much the greater part of this great man!) lives after him and will live for ever.

—Lord Alfred Douglas, "The Genius of
Oscar Wilde," *Academy,* July 11, 1908, p. 35

G.K. Chesterton "Oscar Wilde" (1909)

G.K. Chesterton was an English polymath of the early twentieth century, a journalist, political philosopher, and author of fantasy and detective stories, Christian apologetics, and poetry. In this extract, Chesterton reveals his eye for nuance, breaking down seeming contradictions into a unified interpretation of Wilde's art.

Chesterton recognizes that, by the time he is writing the following extract, Wilde's criminal conviction was no longer a necessary bar to appreciating his art. The fact that Wilde had been punished for his offences against English moral opinion allows him to be considered simply and straightforwardly as a "man of letters." Indeed, Chesterton cleverly suggests that it is precisely because Wilde had been sacrificed on the altar of the English public's indignation that his appreciation as an artist is now made possible. He amusingly writes that "Any ox that is really sacrificed is made sacred."

Chesterton takes issue with the perception of the great artist as being the opposite of the charlatan. He sees Wilde as both, defining a charlatan as one who is fully aware of the clever illusions he sports before his audiences while retaining a sense of disgust for the very conjurations he performs. Chesterton sees in Wilde's dramas evidence of both his greatness as an artist and also this chicanery, examining various witty epigrams as evidence of one or the other.

In examining the "spiritual" side of Wilde, Chesterton remarks that simply by attempting to access all possible personalities, adopting them here and there according to aesthetic whim, Wilde inevitably displayed the spiritual side of man. Chesterton suggests that Wilde's fallacy was that he did not appreciate that, in attempting to be all things at one time or another, certain attitudes negated the possibility of others. One cannot be an innocent if one has dabbled in the posturing of the wicked. It is a sensitive and subtle analysis of Wilde's moral position and the logical consequences of an aesthetic philosophy proposing the artist's adoption of various masks and a multifaceted identity.

The time has certainly come when this extraordinary man, Oscar Wilde, may be considered merely as a man of letters. He sometimes pretended that art was more important than morality, but that was mere play-acting. Morality or immorality was more important than art to him and everyone else. But the very cloud of tragedy that rested on his career makes it easier to treat him as a mere artist now. His was a complete life, in that awful sense in which your life and mine are incomplete; since we have not yet paid for our sins. In that sense one might call it a perfect life, as one speaks of a perfect equation; it cancels out. On the one hand we have the healthy horror of the evil; on the other the healthy horror of the punishment. We have it all the more because both sin and punishment were highly civilized; that is, nameless and secret. Some have said that Wilde was sacrificed; let it be enough for us to insist on the literal meaning of the word. Any ox that is really sacrificed is made sacred.

But the very fact that monstrous wrong and monstrous revenge cancel each other, actually does leave this individual artist in that very airy detachment which he professed to desire. We can really consider him solely as a man of letters.

About Oscar Wilde, as about other wits, Disraeli or Bernard Shaw, men wage a war of words, some calling him a great artist and others a mere charlatan. But this controversy misses the really extraordinary thing about Wilde: the thing that appears rather in the plays than the poems. He was a great artist. He also was really a charlatan. I mean by a charlatan one sufficiently dignified to despise the tricks that he employs. A vulgar demagogue is not a charlatan; he is as coarse as his crowd. He may be lying in every word, but he is sincere in his style. Style (as Wilde might have said) is only another name for spirit. Again, a man like Mr. Bernard Shaw is not a charlatan. I can understand people thinking his remarks hurried or shallow or senselessly perverse, or blasphemous, or merely narrow. But I cannot understand anyone railing to feel that Mr. Shaw is being as suggestive as he can, is giving his brightest and boldest speculations to the rabble, is offering something which he honestly thinks valuable. Now Wilde often uttered remarks which he must have known to be literally valueless. Shaw may be high or low, but he never talks down to the audience. Wilde did talk down, sometimes very far down.

Wilde and his school professed to stand as solitary artistic souls apart from the public. They professed to scorn the middle class, and declared that the artist must not work for the bourgeois. The truth is that no artist so really great ever worked so much for the bourgeois as Oscar Wilde. No man, so capable of thinking about truth and beauty, ever thought so constantly about his own effect on the middle classes. He studied them with exquisite attention, and knew exactly how to shock and how to please them. Mr. Shaw often gets above them in seraphic indignation, and often below them in sterile and materialistic explanations. He disgusts them with new truths or he bores them with old truths; but they are always living truths to Bernard Shaw. Wilde knew how to say the precise thing which, whether true or false, is irresistible. As, for example, "I can resist everything but temptation."

But he sometimes sank lower. One might go through his swift and sparkling plays with a red and blue pencil marking two kinds of epigrams; the real epigram which he wrote to please his own wild intellect, and the sham epigram which he wrote to thrill the very tamest part of our tame civilization. This is what I mean by saying that he was strictly a charlatan— among other things. He descended below himself to be on top of others. He became purposely stupider than Oscar Wilde that he might seem cleverer than the nearest curate. He lowered himself to superiority; he stooped to conquer.

One might easily take examples of the phrase meant to lightly touch the truth and the phrase meant only to bluff the bourgeoisie. For instance, in A *Woman of No Importance,* he makes his chief philosopher say that all thought is immoral, being essentially destructive; "Nothing survives being thought of." That is nonsense, but nonsense of the nobler sort; there is an idea in it. It is, like most professedly modern ideas, a death-dealing idea not a life-giving one; but it is an idea. There is truly a sense in which all definition is deletion. Turn a few pages of the same play and you will find somebody asking, "What is an immoral woman?" The philosopher answers, "The kind of woman a man never gets tired of." Now that is not nonsense, but rather rubbish. It is without value of any sort or kind. It is not symbolically true; it is not fantastically true; it is not true at all.

Anyone with the mildest knowledge of the world knows that nobody can be such a consuming bore as a certain kind of immoral woman. That vice never tires men, might be a tenable and entertaining lie; that the individual instrument of vice never tires them is not, even as a lie, tenable enough to be entertaining. Here the great wit was playing the cheap dandy to the incredibly innocent; as much as if he had put on paper cuffs and collars. He is simply shocking a tame curate; and he must be rather a specially tame curate even to be shocked. This irritating duplication of real brilliancy with snobbish bluff runs through all his three comedies. "Life is much too important to be taken seriously"; that is the true humorist. "A well-tied tie is the first serious step in life"; that is the charlatan. "Man can believe the impossible, but man can never believe the improbable"; that is said by a fine philosopher. "Nothing is so fatal to a personality as the keeping of promises, unless it be telling the truth"; that is said by a tired quack. "A man can be happy with any woman so long as he does not love her"; that is wild truth. "Good intentions are invariably ungrammatical"; that is tame trash.

But while he had a strain of humbug in him, which there is not in the demagogues of wit like Bernard Shaw, he had, in his own strange way, a much deeper and more spiritual nature than they. Queerly enough, it was the very multitude of his falsities that prevented him from being entirely false. Like a many-coloured humming top, he was at once a bewilderment and a balance. He was so fond of being many-sided that among his sides he even admitted the right side. He loved so much to multiply his souls that he had amongst them one soul at least that was saved. He desired all beautiful things—even God.

His frightful fallacy was that he would not see that there is reason in everything, even in religion and morality. Universality is a contradiction in terms. You cannot be everything if you are anything. If you wish to be white all over, you must austerely resist the temptation to have green spots or yellow stripes. If you wish to be good all over, you must resist the spots of sin or the stripes of servitude. It may be great fun to be many-sided; but however many sides one has there cannot be one of them which is complete and rounded innocence. A polygon can have an infinite number of sides; but no one of its sides can be a circle.

—G.K. Chesterton, "Oscar Wilde," 1909,
A Handful of Authors, ed. Dorothy Collins,
1953, pp. 143–146

James Joyce "Oscar Wilde: The Poet of *Salomé*" (1909)

James Joyce was an Irish novelist, poet, and dramatist and became one of the most influential writers of the twentieth century. In the following extract Joyce considers Wilde's imprisonment and his relationship to the English reading public, the reason that his art caused their resentment and his downfall, and what it meant for the interpretation and reception of Wilde's own literary works. Joyce is, in typical fashion, blunt but insightful when considering Wilde's disgrace before the literary world. The conception of Wilde as a martyr is still very much a prevalent theme in criticism today.

Joyce begins by stating that it was not Wilde's life or moral behavior that brought about his downfall, but that he was of necessity made a scapegoat for the sins of the English themselves. Wilde had said about his novel, *The Picture of Dorian Gray*, that each individual saw in Dorian's unnamed sin his own secret shame. It was the public's own discomfort and the fact that Wilde did not hypocritically hide his "sin," thereby causing a scandal in full view before them, that inevitably prompted their reaction against him.

Joyce reads sin, rather than a desire to return beauty to the world, as lying at the heart of Wilde's work. Only sin, Joyce says, can reveal to man the true sense of separation and loss that leads to the divine. With his imprisonment and the subsequent writing of *De Profundis*, Wilde revealed his real worth beneath the cloak of his sins, the "mantle of Heliogabalus" (an infamous and debauched Roman emperor), as Joyce puts it. The conclusion to the extract makes it clear that Joyce considers Wilde to have been a literary martyr, his works now up for grabs before the same public who brought the artist down in the first place. Joyce references the biblical description of Christ's belongings being gambled over at the site of his crucifixion and suggests the description would be a fitting epitaph not only for Wilde the artist but also for the remnant of his art, rummaged through and grubbily fought for by those same individuals who had claimed the life of its creator.

———

This is not the place to examine the strange problem of the life of Oscar Wilde, nor to determine to what extent heredity and the epileptic tendency of his nervous system can excuse that which has been imputed to him. Whether he was innocent or guilty of the charges brought against him, he undoubtedly was a scapegoat. His greater crime was that he had caused a scandal in England, and it is well known that the English authorities did everything possible to persuade him to flee before they issued an order for his arrest. An employee of the Ministry of Internal Affairs stated during the trial that, in London alone, there are more than 20,000 persons under police surveillance, but they remain footloose until they provoke a scandal. Wilde's letters to his friends were read in court, and their author was denounced as a degenerate obsessed by exotic perversions: 'Time wars against you; it is jealous of your lilies and your roses', 'I love to see you wandering through violet-filled valleys, with your honey-coloured hair gleaming'. But the truth is that Wilde, far from being a perverted monster who sprang in some inexplicable way from the civilization of modern England, is the logical and inescapable product of the Anglo-Saxon college and university system, with its secrecy and restrictions.

Wilde's condemnation by the English people arose from many complex causes; but it was not the simple reaction of a pure conscience. Anyone who scrutinizes the graffiti, the loose drawings, the lewd gestures of those people will hesitate to believe them pure at heart. Anyone who follows closely the life and language of men, whether in soldiers' barracks or in the great commercial houses, will hesitate to believe that all those who threw stones at Wilde were themselves spotless. In fact, everyone feels uncomfortable in speaking to others about this subject, afraid that his listener may know more about it than he does. Oscar Wilde's own defence in the *Scots Observer* should remain valid in the judgment of an objective critic. Everyone, he wrote, sees his own sin in *Dorian Gray* (Wilde's best known novel). What Dorian Gray's sin was no one says and no one knows. Anyone who recognizes it has committed it.

Here we touch the pulse of Wilde's art—sin. He deceived himself into believing that he was the bearer of good news of neo-paganism to an enslaved people. His own distinctive qualities, the qualities, perhaps, of his race— keenness, generosity, and a sexless intellect—he placed at the service of a theory of beauty which, according to him, was to bring back the Golden Age and the joy of the world's youth. But if some truth adheres to his subjective interpretations of Aristotle, to his restless thought that proceeds by sophisms rather than syllogisms, to his assimilations of natures as foreign to his as the delinquent is to the humble, at its very base is the truth inherent in the soul of Catholicism: that man cannot reach the divine heart except through that sense of separation and loss called sin.

In his last book, *De Profundis*, he kneels before a gnostic Christ, resurrected from the apocryphal pages of *The House of Pomegranates*, and then his true soul, trembling, timid, and saddened, shines through the mantle of Heliogabalus. His fantastic legend, his opera—a polyphonic variation on the rapport of art and nature, but at the same time a revelation of his own psyche—his brilliant books sparkling with epigrams (which made him, in the view of some people, the most penetrating speaker of the past century), these are now divided booty.

A verse from the book of Job is cut on his tombstone in the impoverished cemetery at Bagneux. It praises his facility, 'eloquium suum',—the great legendary mantle which is now divided booty. Perhaps the future will also carve there another verse, less proud but more pious:

Partiti sunt sibi vestimenta mea et super
vestem meam miserunt sortis.

—James Joyce, "Oscar Wilde:
The Poet of *Salomé*," 1909, *Critical Writings*,
eds. Ellsworth Mason and Richard Ellmann,
1959, pp. 203–205

LEWIS PIAGET SHANKS "OSCAR WILDE'S PLACE IN LITERATURE" (1910)

Lewis Piaget Shanks was, at the time the following extract was written, a professor of romance languages at the University of Tennessee and later a professor at Johns Hopkins University. *The Dial* was an American journal famous for its promotion of modernism and for publishing the work of a large number of modernist writers. This extract examines Wilde's claim to fame within the canons of literature and is written on the publication of a new, definitive edition of Wilde's works. As Shanks says, the evidence for judging Wilde is now "all in."

Shanks explores the often-made accusation that Wilde plagiarized from a host of other writers' texts and thoughts. He points out that Wilde himself never denied it and had stated that the best of writers were always known for the ways they employed their various borrowing and transformations. Shanks humorously remarks that literature has no Monroe Doctrine (the United States' political doctrine stating that Great Britain should not interfere in the affairs of the then newly founded nations of the Americas) and that perhaps one day, a socialistic, common ownership of past writers would make plagiarism a literary virtue. Shanks recognizes that, like Shakespeare, Wilde's imitation of others is indulged with the hope that other writers will afterward imitate him. The plagiarism of Wilde is still a critical concern today but is now usually seen as part of Wilde's theories on aesthetically re-creating the past, rewriting historical moments, and his use of a series of masks, this time those of other writers and stylists.

Shanks finds little of worth in Wilde's early poetry apart from the sonnets, in which he sees a mastery of technique "second to none" among England's minor poets. But it is, ironically, the "tyranny of technique" that Shanks sees as ultimately restricting Wilde's art. He believes that Wilde was ever in search of a witticism, an epigram, a paradox with which to startle his audience and that this necessarily constricted the development and presentation of his thought. Shanks resorts several times to "what might have been if only . . ." scenarios for Wilde: if he had edited out the "purple patches" of prose (overly ornate and stylized writing), if he had allowed ideas to dictate his style rather than vice versa, if the characters of his dramas and novel had been more emotionally rounded rather than mannered "marionettes." But it is the artificiality of which Shanks complains in Wilde's other work that he believes to be of artistic benefit in the fairy tales. They are charming, and their form matches their content, precisely because they are of little literary weight due to their "slightness of texture." Equally, with Wilde's plays, Shanks believes the frivolous, epigrammatic style does not allow for any serious purpose or moral. But Shanks's problem is with Wilde's style and its inability to lend his art any seriousness or sincerity.

It is only in *De Profundis* that Shanks sees a unity of style and spirit or thought. He finds in the letter certain pages that are "almost beyond criticism." It is this document alone that Shanks is sure will survive as "great art," and he concludes suggesting that the publishers should have brought out not a complete works of Wilde but rather a selection expunged of epigrams. Shanks, ultimately, takes the critical stance that *De Profundis* is sincere (contrast Max Beerbohm's interpretation of the same text in an earlier extract) and that it is Wilde's wit that detracts from his status as a great author. In 1910, in the face of the incipient modernist movement, Wilde's lack of seriousness and his poetic style are, not surprisingly, being critiqued as out of date. It would take some years of distancing for at least the latter to once more be critically appreciated, for there were always those who found Wilde's witticisms appealing. As Shanks admits at the start of his own essay, it may have been "over-early" when he put pen to paper to assess the strength of Wilde's art.

After a decade of noisy oblivion, the writings of Oscar Wilde have received the recognition of a definitive edition, worthy as to form and complete in contents. No longer need we contend with the pornographic stock-broker at the book-auction, or shake our heads over the excessive prices of items listed in the catalogues under the dreadful caption of *Oscariana*. However, no one but the collector will complain that Wilde is no longer a rarity. Now at last we can fight in the light: we may "adopt an attitude," to use a phrase of Wilde's own, toward a definitely presented literary talent; and even the apologists who plead that Villon was a rascal and Shakespeare a poacher, may judge whether or not we shall forget that the "apostle of the English Renaissance" was an improper person.

Will Wilde survive? The answer lies in these substantial volumes; the evidence is all in, though it may be over-early to discuss it. What strikes one first is the range of the writings: there are plays, novels, poems, essays, art-criticism, book-reviews, and autobiography; nothing is lacking but history and the "miscellaneous divinity" of the old-book stores! Wilde preferred making history to writing it (we are still trying to forget the lily!); and if he worshipped Pater's style, he did not care in the least for patristic literature. Here, therefore, we must content ourselves with the Pre-Raphaelite lyrics, filled with aesthetic religiosity as the poems of Dante Gabriel Rossetti: charming decorative pieces surely, but insincere in spirit as most of our modern cathedral glass. Mediaeval feeling, after all, can hardly be reproduced in a copy of a copy.

Rossetti is but one of Wilde's literary models; every great poet of the Victorian age finds a second immortality in his verses. They pass before us in "The Garden of Eros"—Keats, Shelley, Swinburne, Morris, and the poet-painter himself. But if we add to these self-confessed mentors most of the other great English poets, and to these Homer and the Greeks, and Dante, and a few of the lyrists of France, we shall get a better idea of the range of his reading and the strength of his memory. No academic ear is needed to detect this; echo follows echo as in a musical comedy. "The true artist is known," said Wilde in one of his reviews, "by the use he makes of what he annexes; and he annexes everything." So our poet modestly lived up to his maxim, aware that in literature at least there is no Monroe Doctrine. Had not Moliere said, before him, "Je prends mon bien ou je le trouve"? Like Moliere, we are all plagiarists—though hardly, perhaps, with such an excuse; and some Elysian day, when all but the scholars have ceased to read the classics, judicious plagiarism may become a literary virtue, supported by a socialistic culture and justified by the pedagogic theories of Rousseau.

So perhaps might Wilde have justified his imitations. But his plagiarism was of the old-fashioned sturdier sort, like Shakespeare's or Moliere's. He copied from other poets, hoping, as all plagiarists hope, that in the course of time others might copy him. He copied himself, to show that he was not unworthy of the compliment. Did not Homer repeat his adjectives, his similes? So in these books the best refuses to be hidden, and telling epithets, aphorisms, and puns reappear like comets in the cosmic life. Over a score of the epigrams in A *Woman of No Importance* are taken from *Dorian Gray*. Like the bird in Browning's verses, Wilde

> Sings each song twice over,
> Lest you should think he never could recapture
> The first fine careless rapture.

One cannot see how much of the early verse can survive. We soon tire of hydromel, and a Keats devoid of genius becomes the most dreadful of literary diets. Alas for Wilde! he feasted too long on ambrosia, and drank too deeply of his "poppy-seeded wine." To read his verse at all is cloying, and to read much of it is like a literary debauch. The best things are the Sonnets, in which the imagery is definitely limited by the form: there at least the reader is sure of one thought for every fourteen lines. Next to these come, not the "Pagan" verses, far too morbidly romantic to be Greek, but the pastel-like pictures inspired by Gautier, some of which have all the delicate impressionism of *Emaux et camees*. What could be better in its way than this:

LA FUITE DE LA LUNE
To outer senses there is peace,
    A dreamy peace on either hand,
    Deep silence in the shadowy land,
Deep silence where the shadows cease.
Save for a cry that echoes shrill
    From some lone bird disconsolate;
    A corncrake calling to its mate;
The answer from the misty hill.
And suddenly the moon withdraws
    Her sickle from the lightening skies,
    And to her sombre cavern flies,
Wrapped in a veil of yellow gauze.

No minor poet in England ever attained a more thorough mastery of technique than Wilde: we see it in the sonnets, as nearly perfect in construction as the study of Milton could make them; we see it pushed to the extreme of *l'art pour l'art* in that bit of Byzantine mosaic, *The Sphinx*. Yet of these early poems none are to be found in the anthologies save "Ave Imperatrix," which alone catches a breath of national feeling in an adequate chord. Most of them, to be sure, are esoteric; when we read them we wonder what is the matter, but when we have read them we conclude that there isn't any. Never did Wilde conform more closely to his maxim, "Youth is rarely original."

    The Ballad of Reading Gaol was written fifteen years later. We all remember how it was received; we remember—alas!—how it was compared to *The Ancient Mariner*. Such judgments show the evils of literary journalism: they indicate that the critic has had no time to read Coleridge since his college days. *Reading Gaol* has more limp-leather editions to its credit in the department stores,—but where in Wilde's ballad do we find anything like the conception, the imaginative power, and the classic simplicity of *The Ancient Mariner*, whose every sentence is as full of meaning as the etcher's line? *Reading Gaol* does recall Coleridge, as "Charmides" recalls something of

Keats; but the first poem is too brutal, the second too delicately indelicate, to carry out the comparison invited by occasional imitative lines. No realism, however, poignant, can match the serene imaginative reality of the earlier poem; we want no paradoxes in the ballad, we want no ballad so artistic as to be artificial. And, after all, Wilde never forgets that the important thing in his poem is the manner.

The tyranny of technique is Wilde's real prison-wall. If art is not able to effect itself—*ars est celare artem*—better to write without regard for style than use the diction of "The Decay of Lying." Such prose makes one think that it is possible for an artist to be too articulate. "The world was created," said Stephane Mallarme, "in order to lead up to a fine book." For Wilde, apparently, the cosmic processes led up to the paradox. "Pen, Pencil, and Poison" was built around an epigram, and "The Model Millionaire" was written for the sake of a pun. "Paradoxy is my doxy" is the basis of his artistic creed; and the principle of his method is simple contrariety. For example:

> After the death of her third husband her hair
> turned quite gold from grief.
> We live in an age that reads too much to be wise,
> and thinks too much to be beautiful.

What could be simpler than the *modus operandi?* Yet each of these phrases occurs three times in the volumes before us, with many another gem of rare and recurrent wit. Surely Wilde knew that the best of paradoxes will scarce bear repetition, and that the wittiest of epigrams loses its flavor when it becomes a refrain.

The least affected of Wilde's prose is to be found in the journalistic criticism which fills a volume and a half of the collected works; book-reviews of purely ephemeral interest, yet written with sprightly grace and wit, and full of literary judgments which will be turned against their author—when our would-be doctors fall upon the difference between Wilde's preaching and his practice! And to reward their labors, they will find some charming "purple patches"; the best of these were afterwards worked into the pages of *Intentions*. Wilde might have become a critic of importance, had it been given him to outgrow his paradoxes and to chasten his style. He had a nice appreciation of all the arts, and a sense of the melodic possibilities of language that puts his best work beside that of Pater; and, unlike Pater, he never falls from music to mosaic. Truly, *Intentions* is a delightful book,—but how far below Pater, if we consider it as a collection of essays! How far below Landor in its management of the dialogue form! Wilde's adversary is always the man of straw; there is none of the play of personality, the contrast of opposite standpoints, that we find in such books as Mallock's *New Republic*. Wilde could not project himself into the intellectual life of another. This is the fault of all his work. The very types in his plays, excepting those that call for a mere surface characterization, are at heart merely dramatic phases of the moods or poses of their author. He gives them emotions, but not minds or characters; he makes them real by their repartee. They are puppets animated by puns; they bedazzle our judgment with a pyrotechnic shower of epigrams. We are carried away by it all, but we are left nothing which we can carry away. The aesthetic "katharsis" of his dramatic theories is lost sight of; we must purge our souls with paradoxes, and in improper situations make them clean. After all, the characters of these plays are not characters, for all they have the tone of good society. They are sometimes society men and women, but more often only marionettes with manners.

Marionettes, too, are the men and women of *Dorian Gray*. Lord Henry Wotton, brilliant, autobiographic, the monocled Mephisto of an ineffectual Faust, may alone be said to live, and at times the reader finds him more lively than alive. Dorian simply doesn't exist; he has sold his conscience for an eternal youth,—and what man can exist without a conscience? Sybil Vane is a shadow, and the painter Hallward the shadow of a shade. He is never so living as when he is slain, and his corpse sits sprawling in the dreadful attic. Only a few of the minor characters, sketched in, like the unctuous Jew of the theatre, with broad realistic touches, may be said to live even as properties. No, *Dorian Gray* is a good subject spoiled. One can imagine how Flaubert would have told the story, how Balzac would have filled it with fiery-colored life. Yet some have compared this novel to *La Peau de chagrin!*

The shorter stories need not detain us; they are less real than the fairy-tales. We turn with pleasure to *The Happy Prince* and *The House of Pomegranates*,— for the luxuriance that cloys in the poems becomes delightful when submitted to the partial restraint of a poetic prose. No one, of course, would go to Oscar Wilde for the trenchant simplicity of the German folk-tale. His are merely artistic apologues, touching life with the light satire of the drawing-room. One forgets their author, excepting when he is sticking pins into his puppets to create an artistic pathos; only then do we rebel. However, Wilde did not take his heroes seriously, nor need we. Let us be thankful that he does not, that he drags in no pompous moral, for without it these fables have all the honesty of the frankly artificial, and in their very slightness of texture lies the secret of their charm.

The case is the same with the plays. The best of the comedies have a sort of frivolous unity; they are often terribly affected, but they never affect a moral. Sincerity makes Wilde inconsistent with his art; he becomes impossible when he assumes a purpose, and intolerable when he has a paradox to prove. Could anything be worse than the essay on Socialism? But no problems spoil his plays, and when we find that the least serious of them is incomparably the best, the inference is easy. He felt too much the charm of his material; he found it easier to play with constructions than to construct a play. As a follower of *l'art pour l'art*, a purpose would spoil him, and he admitted sincerity only in his attitude toward aesthetics. Yet the value of a fundamental seriousness is nowhere more apparent than in the superiority of his art-lectures to such work as "Pen, Pencil, and Poison."

The final necessity of subduing style and spirit in a deeper unity is shown in *De Profundis*. Reading Gaol, and not Oxford, gave us the final development of Wilde's prose. It is said that prisons make men liars; but it was none the less a prison that made *De Profundis* sincere. Here first his art attains its final unity,—a unity of spirit and form which puts certain pages of his confession almost beyond criticism. All of his early work, in comparison, seems little more than a promise; for here alone he attains the simplicity of great art.

When we add to this its value as a "document," we cannot doubt that *De Profundis* will survive. It is a pity that this is all we can be sure of. But *The Ballad of Reading Gaol* contains too much alloy; if it becomes a classic our classics will have lived. The art-criticism, the aesthetic "philosophy," will be stolen and rewritten, as it was originally stolen and rewritten by Wilde. The life of the plays is limited by the life of their paradoxes, as we can see from the puns in Shakespeare; and even the fairy tales need more human nature to keep them alive. Wilde's place in literature, in so far as he concerns us, is that of a precursor: he prepared the way for Shaw's paradoxes, and the success of Chesterton is to be laid at his door. He revealed to us a certain kind of wit, but he has made some of our critics tremendously trifling. Everything considered, Wilde's literary executors would have done better to give us a selection from his works—a careful selection, with all the cheapest epigrams expunged. Not even a reviewer can read a dozen volumes of this sort with impunity!

—Lewis Piaget Shanks, "Oscar Wilde's
Place in Literature," *Dial*, April 16,
1910, pp. 261–263

ARCHIBALD HENDERSON (1911)

Archibald Henderson describes Wilde as a "pointilliste," referring to the late-nineteenth-century style of painting in which small points of primary colors, when viewed from a distance, suggest secondary colors and various tonal nuances. In other words, Henderson contends that Wilde is an artist who must be viewed from just the right angle in order to appreciate the "whole" of his art. In this extract, Henderson assesses the pointilliste style as giving only the "appearance" of a whole.

The almost impossible task of critically considering Wilde's art as a unified whole is tied up for Henderson with the question of Wilde's own character. He states that it is dangerous to unequivocally associate a man's personal life with his art, describing Wilde as a "pervert and a degenerate" while some of his poetry is possessed of "the divine spark." While Henderson accepts that some of Wilde's art was indeed "irresponsible" and "dangerous," he also believes that certain "exquisite truths" are evident amid "damnably perverse falsehood." But it is Wilde's capacity to adopt the personalities and perspectives of others, to see life through new eyes (an ability Henderson believes at the time he was writing to be almost a lost art), that is chiefly to Wilde's credit. By multiplying his own personality, he multiplied the perspectives found within his art.

Wilde was, in his own phrase, the "critic as artist" rather than, for Henderson, a creator himself. It was the critical assessment, through the lens of his aestheticism, of life and others' art that was the source of Wilde's genius. In commenting on Wilde's drama, Henderson suggests that it was the passion for art itself that was Wilde's chief strength. Life, truth, and humanity were of little importance in his staged works. It is precisely because of the many perspectives adopted by Wilde that his aesthetic never promoted viewing the world as a "whole." Rather Wilde's art is produced in the manner of the pointilliste, in singular and shifting points of color: Dazzling though they may have sometimes been, they give only the suggestion of unity.

—◦◦◦—   —◦◦◦—   —◦◦◦—

At bottom and in essence, Wilde is a master in the art of selection. He is eminently successful in giving the most diverting character to our moments as they pass. His art is the apotheosis of the moment. What may not be said, he once asked, for the moment and the "moment's monument"? Art itself, he averred, is "really a form of exaggeration, and selection, which is the very spirit of art, is nothing more than an intensified mode of over-emphasis." Wilde was a painter, a Neo-Impressionist. From the palette of his observation, which bore all the radiant shades and colors of his temperament, he selected and laid upon the canvas many brilliant yet distinct points of color. Seen in the proper light and from the just distance, the canvas takes on the appearance of a complete picture—quaint, unique, marvellous. It is only by taking precisely Wilde's point of view that the spectator is enabled to synthesize the isolated brilliant points into a harmonious whole. Oscar Wilde is a Pointilliste.

There is no room for doubt that Oscar Wilde was, as Nordau classed him, a pervert and a degenerate. And yet his case warrants distrust of the dictum that an artist's work and life are fundamentally indissociable. Wilde was a man, not only of multiple personality, but of manifest and disparate achievement. The style is not always the man; and the history of art and literature reveals not a few geniuses whose private life could not justly be cited in condemnation of their pictures, their poetry, or their prose. If Wilde's life were to be cited as the sole criterion of his works, then must they forever remain *res tacenda* in the republic of letters. It is indubitable that Wilde, with his frequently avowed doctrine of irresponsible individualism and Pagan insistence upon the untrammelled expansion of the Ego, gave suicidal counsel to the younger generation. He based his apostolate upon the paradox; and as he himself asserts, the paradox is always dangerous. In his search for the elusive, the evanescent, the imaginative, he found certain exquisite truths; but they were only very partial and obscure truths, embedded in a mass of charmingly phrased, yet damnably perverse, falsehood. Much of his verse—flagrant output of what Robert Buchanan maliciously crystallized in the damning phrase, "The Fleshly School of Poetry"—is a faithful reflex of his personality and feeling, with its morbid and sensuous daydreams, its vain regrets for "barren gain and bitter loss," its unhealthy and myopic vision, its obsession with the wanton and the *macabre*. And yet, in spite not only of these things but also of the persistent reminder of alien influences, certain of his poems are lit with the divine spark and fitfully flame out with startling and disturbing lustre.

As an artist in words, as *prosateur,* Wilde was possessed of real gifts. The social ease of his paradoxes, the opulence of his imaginative style, the union of simplicity and beauty of phraseology with vague and sometimes almost meaningless gradations and shades of thought, his insight into the real meaning of art, his understanding of the "thing as in itself it really is," and his rapt glimpses of art's holy of holies—all these things, at times and at intervals, were his. His faculty of imitation was caricature refined and sublimated to an infinite degree; and, with less real comprehension of the *arcana* of art, Wilde might have been the author of a transcendent *Borrowed Plumes*. And if he himself did not actually and literally masquerade in the literary garments of other men, certainly he possessed that rare faculty, now almost a lost art, of creeping into another's personality, temporarily shedding the husk of self, and looking out upon the world with new and alien eyes. There lies, it would seem, the secret of his genius—the faculty of creative and imaginative interpretation in its ultimate refinement. He was ever the critic as artist, never the creator in the fine frenzy of creation. It has been said of him that he knew everything; but in the last analysis his supreme fault, both as man and artist, was his arrogance and his overweening sense of superiority. Breaks down in Wilde's case—as does many another truism—the maxim: *Tout comprendre c'est tout pardonner.*

"To be free," wrote a celebrity, "one must not conform." Wilde secured a certain sort of freedom in the drama through his refusal to conform to the laws of dramatic art. He claimed the privileges without shouldering the responsibilities of the dramatist. He imported the methods of the *causerie* into the domain of the drama, and turned the theatre into a house of mirth. Whether or no his destination was the palace of truth, certain it is that he always stopped at the half-way house. Art was the dominant note of his literary life; but it was the art of conversation, not the art of drama. His comedies, as dramas, were cheap sacrifices to the god of success. He made many delightful, many pertinent and impertinent observations upon English life, and upon life in general; but they had no special relation to the dramatic theme he happened for the moment to have in mind. His plays neither enlarge the mental horizon nor dilate the heart. Wilde was too self-centred an egoist ever to come into any real or vital relation with life. It was his primal distinction as artist to be consumed with a passionate love of art. It was his primal deficiency as artist to have no genuine sympathy with humanity. And although he imaged life with clearness, grace, and distinction, certain it is that he never saw life steadily, nor ever saw it whole.

Wilde called one of his plays *The Importance of Being Earnest*. In his inverted way, he aimed at teaching the world the importance of being frivolous. Only from this standpoint is it possible to appreciate, in any real sense, Wilde the comic dramatist. Wilde is the arch enemy of boredom and ennui; we can always enjoy him in his *beau role* as a purveyor of amusement and a killer of time. But we are warned by his own confession against taking Wilde, as dramatist, too seriously. "The plays are not great," he once confessed to Andre Gide. "I think nothing of them—but if you only knew how amusing they are!" And the author of "The Decay of Lying" added: "Most of them are the results of bets"!

—Archibald Henderson, *Interpreters of Life and the Modern Spirit*, 1911, pp. 99–103

ARTHUR RANSOME
"AFTERTHOUGHT" (1912)

Arthur Ransome was an English author and journalist, today most famous for his children's classic *Swallows and Amazons*. The book from which the following extract is taken embroiled Ransome in a lawsuit, brought against him by Alfred Douglas for comments made about Douglas's sexual relationship with Wilde. Ransome would win the case.

Ransome examines what is meant when critics have spoken of Wilde's "poses." He rightly states that in Wilde's case, the word *pose* was not applicable in the sense of pretending but rather in the sense of his forthright presentation of himself before the public. Wilde was aware of his artistic and intellectual distinction, and Ransome contrasts Poe's scorn of those he considered as less able to intuit Wilde's natural charm and inherent generosity to those same types. Against the critical view that claimed Wilde was a fake, Ransome states that he was no charlatan, for he was always capable of delivering what he promised.

Ransome considers the three things that have been left by Wilde to posterity: his legend, his words, and his works. Of the first, Ransome cannily suggests that the dramatic events surrounding Wilde's imprisonment will be reinterpreted in times to come; the second, Wilde's conversation, is admiringly described as being akin to a dazzling tapestry of effect, a magical kaleidoscope of embroideries and shifting focuses; finally, Wilde's works are described as the product of an idle but brilliant man, consummately playing with the presentation of ideas in his moments of leisure. For Ransome, Wilde's recreational approach to his art is suggested as being perhaps Wilde's sole regret at the end of his life: He might have achieved a much more worthy memorial to his artistic powers.

Ransome's analysis is intelligent, sympathetic, and forward looking. The critical division of Wilde's life from his conversation, and of each from his works, is not, even today, an uncommon critical approach. Ransome recognizes, as the best critics of Wilde have done, that it is a unique credit to the man that his life was of such dramatic intensity, his conversation

so wittily artistic, and his works a combination of that drama, wit, and art
that each, in a manner unparalleled in the history of English literature,
has become an area of critical study.

—◊◊◊— —◊◊◊— —◊◊◊—

There is a word, often applied to Wilde in his lifetime, that has, since his death, been used to justify a careless neglect of his work. That word is "pose." In all such popular characterizations there is hidden a distorted morsel of truth. Such a morsel of truth is hidden here. We need not examine the dull envy of brilliance, the envy felt by timid persons of a man who dared to display the hopes and the intentions that were making holiday within him, the envy that used that word as a reproach, and sought to veil the fact that it was a confession. But we shall do well to discover what it was beside that envy that made the word applicable to Wilde.

Wilde "posed" as an aesthete. He was an aesthete. He "posed" as brilliant. He was brilliant. He "posed" as cultured. He was cultured. The quality in him to which that word was applied was not pretence, though that was willingly suggested, but display. Wilde let people see, as soon as he could, and in any way that was possible, who and what he was or wished to be. No bushel hid his lamp. He arranged it where it could best be seen, and beat drums before it to summon the spectators. He had every quality of a charlatan, except one: the inability to keep his promises. Wilde promised nothing that he could not perform. But, because he promised so loudly, he earned the scorn of those whom charlatans do not outwit. He has even met with the scorn of charlatans, who cannot understand why he made so much noise when he really could do what he promised.

The noise and the display that were inseparable from any stage of Wilde's career, and were not without an indirect echo and repetition in his books, were partly due to the self-consciousness that was among his most valuable assets. He knew himself, and he knew his worth, and, conscious of an intellectual pre-eminence over most of his fellows, assumed its recognition, and was in a hurry to bring the facts level with his assumption. He had, more than most men, a dramatic conception of himself. "There is a fatality," says the painter of Dorian Gray, "about all physical and intellectual distinction, the sort of fatality that seems to dog the faltering steps of kings. It is better not to be different from one's fellows." Wilde was always profoundly conscious of his own "physical and intellectual distinction," not with the almost scornful consciousness of Poe, but with a deprecating pride and a sense of what was due to it from himself and from others. Wilde's "pose"—call it what you will—is easily adopted by talent since Wilde created it with genius. Its origin was a sense of the possession of genius, of being distinct from the rest of the world. Poe emphasized this distinction by looking at people from a distance. Wilde emphasized it by charming them, with a kind of desperate generosity. He knew that he had largesse to scatter, and not till the end of his life did he begin to feel that he had wasted it, that in him a vivid personality had passed through the world and was not leaving behind it a worthy memorial. This was not the common regret at having been unable to accomplish things. It was a regret at leaving insufficient proof of a power of accomplishment that he did not doubt, but had never exerted to the uttermost. In thinking of the virtuosity of Wilde's manner, a thing not at all common in English literature, we must remember the consciousness of power that wrapped his days in a bright light, served him sometimes as a mantle of invisibility, and made him loved and hated with equal vehemence. His tasks were always too easy for him. He never strained for achievement, and nothing requires more generosity to forgive than success without effort.

This consciousness of his power excused in him an extravagance that in a lesser man would have been laughable. He would have it recognized at all costs, for confirmation's sake. He needed admiration at once, from the world, from England, from London, from any small company in which he happened to be. The same desires whose gratification earned him the epithet "poseur," made him expend in conversation energies that would have multiplied many times the volume if not the value of his writings. He pawned much of himself to the moment, and was never able to redeem it.

He leaves three things behind him, a legend, his conversation, and his works. The legend will be that of a beautiful boy, so gifted that all things were possible to him, so brilliant that in middle age men still thought him young, stepping through imaginary fields of lilies and poisonous irises, and finding the flowers turned suddenly to dung, and his feet caught in a quagmire not only poisonous but ugly. It will include the less intimate horror of a further punishment, an imprisonment without the glamour of murder, as with Wainewright, or that of burglary, as with Deacon Brodie, but a hideous publication to the world of the sordid transformation of those imagined flowers. The lives of Villon and of a few saints can alone show such swift passage from opulence to wretchedness, from ease to danger, from the world to a cell. We are not here concerned to blame or palliate the deeds that made this catastrophe possible, but only to remark that to Wilde himself, in comparison with the life of his intellect, they probably seemed infinitely unimportant and insignificant. The life of the thinker is in thought, of the artist in art. He feels it almost unfair that mere actions should be forced into a position where they have power over his destiny. As time goes on, the legend will, no doubt, be modified. It is too dramatic to be easily forgotten.

In earlier chapters I have spoken of the conversational quality of Wilde's prose, but not, so far, of his conversation, which, to some of those who knew him best, seemed more valuable than the echo of it in his books. It varied at different periods and in different companies. More than one writer has described it, and the descriptions do not agree. With an audience that he thought stupid he was startling, said extravagant things and asked impossible questions. With another, he would trace an idea through history, filling out the facts he needed for his argument with bright pageants of colour, like the paragraphs *of Intentions*. At one dinner-table he discoursed; at another he told stories. Wilde "ne causait pas; il contait," says M. Gide. He spoke in parables, and, as he was an artist, he made more of the parables than of their meanings. An idea of this fairy-tale talk may be gathered from his *Poems in Prose*. These things, among the most wonderful that Wilde wrote, are said to be less beautiful in their elaborate form than as he told them over the dinner-table, suggested by the talk that passed. They are certainly a little heavy with gold and precious stones. They are wistful, like princesses in fairy-tales who look out on the world from under their crowns, when other children toss their hair in the wind. But we may well fail to imagine the conversation in which such anecdotes could have a part, not as excrescences but one in texture with the rest. No other English talker has talked in this style, and the Queen Scheherazada did not surpass it when she talked to save her life. Beside Lamb's stuttered jests, Hazlitt's incisions, Coleridge's billowy eloquence, Wilde's tapestried speech must be set among the regrettable things of which time has carelessly deprived us. I have heard it said that Wilde talked for effect. The peacock spreads his tail in burning blue and gold against the emerald lawn, and as Whistler made a room of it, so Wilde made conversation. He talked less to say than to make, and his manner is suggested by his own description of the talk of Lord Henry Wotton in *The Picture of Dorian Gray:—*

"He played with the idea, and grew wilful; tossed it into the air and transformed it; let it escape and recaptured it; made it iridescent with fancy, and winged it with paradox. The praise of folly, as he went on, soared into a philosophy, and Philosophy herself became young, and catching the mad music of Pleasure, wearing, one might fancy, her wine-stained robe and wreath of ivy, danced like a Bacchante over the hills of life, and mocked the slow Silenus for being sober. Facts fled before her like frightened forest things. Her white feet trod the huge press at which wise Omar sits, till the seething grape-juice rose round her bare limbs in waves of purple bubbles, or crawled in red foam over the vat's black, dripping, sloping sides. It was an extraordinary improvisation."

Wilde improvised like that. A metaphor would suddenly grow more important in his eyes than the idea that had called it into being. The idea would vanish in the picture; the picture would elaborate itself and become story, and then, dissolving like a pattern in a kaleidoscope, turn to idea again, and allow him to continue on his way. Wilde talked tapestries, as he wrote them. He saw his conversation, and made other men see it. They thought him a magician. . . .

Wilde provides us with the rare spectacle of a man most of whose powers are those of a spectator, a connoisseur, a man for whom pictures are painted and books written, the perfect collaborator for whom the artist hopes in his heart; the spectacle of such a man, delighting in the delicacies of life no less than in those of art, and yet able to turn the pleasures of the dilettante and the amateur into the motives of the artist. In some ages, when talk has been more highly valued than in ours, he would have been ready to let his criticism die in the air: he would have been content that all who knew him should credit him with the power of doing wonderful things if he chose, and with the preference of touching with the tips of his fingers the baked and painted figurine over the modelling of it in cold and sticky clay. Such credit is not to be had in our time, and he had to take the clay in his fingers and prove his mastery. Besides, he had not the money that would have let him live at ease among blue china, books wonderfully bound, and men and women as strange as the moods it would have pleased him to induce. If he had been rich, I think it possible that he would have been a des Esseintes or a Dorian Gray, and left nothing but a legend and a poem or two, and a few curiosities of luxury to find their way into the sale-rooms.

Wilde preserved, even in those of his writings that cost him most dearly, a feeling of recreation. His books are those of a wonderfully gifted and accomplished man who is an author only in his moments of leisure. Only one comparison is possible, and that is with Horace Walpole; but Wilde's was infinitely the richer intellect. Walpole is weighted by his distinction. Wilde wears his like a flower. Walpole is without breadth, or depth, and equals only as a gossip Wilde's enchanting freedom as a juggler with ideas. Wilde was indolent and knew it. Indolence was, perhaps, the only sin that stared him in the face as he lay dying, for it was the only one that he had committed with a bad conscience. It had lessened his achievement, and left its marks on what he had done. Even in his best work he is sometimes ready to secure an effect too easily. "Meredith is a prose Browning, and so is Browning," may be regarded as an example of such effects. Much of his work fails; much of it has faded, but *Intentions, The Sphinx, The Ballad of Reading Gaol, Salomé, The Importance of Being Earnest,* one or two of the fairy tales, and *De Profundis,* are surely enough with which to challenge the attention of posterity.

These things were the toys of a critical spirit, of a critic as artist, of a critic who took up first one and then another form of art, and played with it almost idly, one and then another form of thought, and gave it wings for the pleasure of seeing it in the light; of a man of action with the eyes of a child; of a man of contemplation curious of all the secrets of life, not only of those that serve an end; of a virtuoso with a distaste for the obvious and a delight in disguising subtlety behind a mask of the very obvious that he disliked. His love for the delicate and the rare brought him into the power of things that are vulgar and coarse. His attempt to weave his life as a tapestry clothed him in a soiled and unbeautiful reality. Even this he was able to subdue. *Nihil tetigit quod non ornavit.* He touched nothing that he did not decorate. He touched nothing that he did not turn into a decoration.

I do not care to prophesy which in particular of these decorations, of these friezes and tapestries of vision and thought, will enjoy that prolongation of life, insignificant in the eternal progress of time, which, for us, seems immortality. Art is, perhaps, our only method of putting off death's victory, but what does it matter to us if the books that feed the intellectual life of our generation are stones to the next and manna to the generation after that? Of this, at least, we may be sure: whether remembered or no, the works that move us now will have an echo that cannot be denied them, unheard but still disturbing, or, perhaps, carefully listened for and picked out, among the myriad roaring of posterity along the furthest and least imaginable corridors of time.

—Arthur Ransome, from "Afterthought,"
Oscar Wilde: A Critical Study, 1912, pp. 220–234

HOLBROOK JACKSON
"OSCAR WILDE: THE LAST PHASE" (1913)

Holbrook Jackson was a literary historian and editor, and this extract is taken from his influential history of the 1890s. In many ways, Jackson might be regarded as the biographer of that decade. His views on Wilde certainly were extraordinarily influential on future critics, especially

Jackson's comments on the importance of critically appreciating the fundamental nature of the relationship between Wilde's character and his art.

Jackson begins by examining Wilde's life, from his meteoric arrival on the literary scene, through the years when he seemed to have achieved a reputation without actually accomplishing anything worthy of fame, to the swift succession of a number of published volumes in the early 1890s, when Wilde seemed to be finally living up to the artistic expectations that had surrounded him for years. Jackson continues tracing Wilde's life, detailing his imprisonment, release, and subsequent exile and death on the Continent, before turning to an examination of those texts that Wilde had published and the question of the situation of his literary reputation more than a decade after his untimely demise. Jackson recognizes that by the mid-1910s, common critical assumption was that, as time passes and the memory of Wilde's life and downfall recede, a more objective appreciation of the man's art may be possible. But Jackson suggests otherwise: It is Wilde's life that is the essential component to understanding his art. The dandyism Wilde represented in both his art and life is considered by Jackson to be the common denominator that all critics must negotiate. Since Wilde believed that art was a vehicle for personality and that one's own life should be a work of art, Jackson focuses on a playful collapsing of usually accepted boundaries between the aesthetic and the real in this extract. Detailing each major event in Wilde's life, Jackson continues to catalog each development in his art. It is an obligatory method for Jackson, for his chapter refuses to recognize, as Wilde himself equally refused to do, a discrete difference between the two.

The singularity of Oscar Wilde has puzzled writers since his death quite as much as it puzzled the public during the startled years of his wonderful visit to the glimpses of Philistia; for after all that has been written about him we are no nearer a convincing interpretation of his character than we were during the great silence which immediately followed his trial and imprisonment. Robert H. Sherard's *Oscar Wilde: The Story of an Unhappy Friendship* throws the clear light of sincerity and eloquence upon his own and his subject's capacity for friendship, but little more than that; André Gide has created a delightful, literary miniature which must always hang on the line in any gallery of studies of Oscar Wilde, but his work is portraiture rather than interpretation. For the rest, we have to be content with such indications of character as may be obtained from the numerous critical essays which have been published during the last few years, notable among them being Arthur Ransome's fine study, and the always wise commentations of Wilde's literary executor and editor, Robert Ross, and the notes and collectanea of Stuart Mason. But whatever ultimate definition his character may assume in future biography, and however difficult such definition may be, it is not so hard to define Oscar Wilde's position and influence during the last decade of the nineteenth century, and what proved to be as well the last decade of his own life.

In the year 1889 Oscar Wilde might have passed away without creating any further comment than that which is accorded an eccentric poet who has succeeded in drawing attention to himself and his work by certain audacities of costume and opinion. His first phase was over, and he had become an outmoded apostle of an aestheticism which had already taken the place of a whimsically remembered fad, a fad which, even then, almost retained only its significance through the medium of Gilbert and Sullivan's satirical opera, *Patience*. He was the man who had evoked merriment by announcing a desire to live up to his blue-and-white china; he was the man who had created a sort of good-humoured indignation by expressing displeasure with the Atlantic Ocean; 'I am not exactly pleased with the Atlantic,' he had confessed. 'It is not so majestic as I expected'; and whose later dissatisfaction with Niagara Falls convinced the United States of America of his flippancy: 'I was disappointed with Niagara. Most people must be disappointed with Niagara. Every American bride is taken there, and the sight of the stupendous waterfall must be one of the earliest if not the keenest disappointments in American married life.' These sayings were beginning to be remembered dimly, along with the picturesque memories of a plum-coloured velveteen knickerbocker suit and a famous stroll down Bond Street as a form of aesthetic propaganda by example. This memory also was aided by W. S. Gilbert:

If you walk down Piccadilly
With a poppy or a lily
In your mediaeval hand. . . .

But certain encounters with Whistler, in which Oscar Wilde felt the sting of the Butterfly, were remembered more distinctly and with more satisfaction, with the result that, besides being outmoded, he became soiled by the charge of plagiarism. 'I wish I had said that, ' he remarked once, approving of one of Whistler's witticisms. 'You will, Oscar; you will!' was the reply. And still more emphatic, the great painter had said on another occasion: 'Oscar has the courage of the opinions . . . of others!' The fact was that the brilliant Oxford graduate had not yet fulfilled the promise of his youth, of his first book, and of his own witty audacity. He had achieved notoriety without fame, and literary reputation without a sufficient means of livelihood, and so small was his position in letters that, from 1887 to 1889, we find him eking out a living by editing *The Woman's World* for Messrs Cassell & Co.

His successes during this period were chiefly in the realms of friendship, and of this the public knew nothing. Publicly he was treated with amiable contempt: he was a social jester, an intellectual buffoon, a poseur; food for the self-righteous laughter of the Philistines; fair quarry for the wits of *Punch*, who did not miss their chance. Yet during the very years he was controlling editorial destinies which were more than foreign to his genius, he was taking the final preparatory steps towards the attractive and sometimes splendid literary output of his last decade. During 1885 and 1890 his unripe genius was feeling its way ever surer and surer towards that mastery of technique and increasing thoughtfulness which afterwards displayed themselves. This was a period of transition and co-ordination. Oscar Wilde was evolving out of one *bizarrerie* and passing into another. And in this evolution he was not only shedding plumes borrowed from Walter Pater, Swinburne and Whistler, he was retaining such of them as suited his needs and making them definitely his own. But, further than that, he was shedding his purely British masters and allowing himself to fall more directly under the influence of a new set of masters in France, where he was always at home, and where he had played the 'sedulous ape' to Balzac some years earlier. From time to time during these years he had polished and engraved and added to the luxuriant imagery of that masterpiece of ornate poetry, *The Sphinx*, which was published in 1894 in a beautiful format with decorations by Charles Ricketts. Essays like 'The Truth of Masks' and 'Shakespeare and Stage Costume' appeared in the pages of *The Nineteenth Century* in 1885; in other publications appeared such stories as 'The Sphinx without a Secret,' 'The Canterville Ghost' and 'Lord Arthur Savile's Crime,' and in 1888 he issued *The Happy Prince and Other Tales*. 'Pen, Pencil and Poison' appeared in *The Fortnightly Review* in 1889, and in the same year *The Nineteenth Century* published the first of his two great colloquies, The *Decay of Lying*. In all of these stories and essays his style was conquering its weaknesses and achieving the undeniable distinction which made him the chief force of the renaissance of the early Nineties. In 1890 his finest colloquy, 'The Critic as Artist,' appeared in *The Nineteenth Century*. Several of the above-named essays and tales went to the making of two of his most important books, *The House of Pomegranates* and *Intentions*, both of which appeared in the first year of the Nineties, and in the same year he published in book form the complete version of *The Picture of Dorian Gray*, thirteen chapters of which had appeared serially in *Lippincott's Monthly Magazine* in the previous year.

Thus, with the dawn of the Eighteen Nineties, Oscar Wilde came into his own. *The House of Pomegranates* alone was sufficient to establish his reputation as an artist, but the insouciant attitude of the paradoxical philosopher revealed in *The Picture of Dorian Gray* and *Intentions* stung waning interest in the whilom apostle of beauty to renewed activity. Shaking off the astonishing reputation which had won him early notoriety as the posturing advertiser of himself by means of the ideas of others, he arose co-ordinate and resplendent, an individual and an influence. He translated himself out of a subject for anecdote into a subject for discussion. And whilst not entirely abandoning that art of personality which had brought him notoriety as a conversationalist and dandy in *salon* and drawing-room and at the dinner-table, he transmuted the personality thus cultivated into the more enduring art of literature, and that brought him fame of which notoriety is but the base metal. For many years he had looked to the theatre as a further means of expression and financial gain, and he had tried his 'prentice hand on the drama with *Vera: or the Nihilists* in 1882, which was produced unsuccessfully in America in 1883, and with *The Duchess of Padua*, written for Mary Anderson and rejected by her about the same time, and produced without encouraging results in New York in 1891. There were also two other early plays, *A Florentine Tragedy*, a fragment only of which remains, and *The Woman Covered with Jewels*, which seems to have been entirely lost. The failure of these works to make any sort of appeal involves no reflection on the public, as they are the veriest stuff of the amateur and imitator; echoes of Sardou and Scribe; romantic costume plays inspired by the theatre rather than by life, and possessing none of the signs of that skilled craftsmanship upon which the merely stage-carpentered play must necessarily depend. But with that change in the whole bent of his genius which heralded the first year of the Nineties came a change also in his skill as a playwright. In 1891 he wrote *Salomé* in French, afterwards translated into English by Lord Alfred Douglas and published by the Bodley Head, with illustrations by Aubrey Beardsley, in 1894. This play would have been produced at the Palace Theatre in 1892 with Madame Sarah Bernhardt in the cast, had not the censor intervened. Oscar Wilde achieved his first dramatic success with *Lady Windermere's Fan*, produced by George Alexander at the St James's Theatre, on 20th February 1892. The success was immediate. Next year Herbert Beerbohm Tree produced *A Woman of No Importance* at the Haymarket Theatre to even more enthusiastic audiences. In 1895 *An Ideal*

Husband was produced at the same theatre in January, and, in February, *The Importance of Being Earnest* was produced at the St. James's.

Oscar Wilde had now reached the age of forty-one and the height of his fame and power. 'The man who can dominate a London dinner-table can dominate the world,' he had said. He had dominated many a London dinner-table; he now dominated the London stage. He was a monarch in his own sphere, rich, famous, popular; looked up to as a master by the younger generation, courted by the fashionable world, loaded with commissions by theatrical managers, interviewed, paragraphed and pictured by the Press, and envied by the envious and the impotent. All the flattery and luxury of success were his, and his luxuriant and applause-loving nature appeared to revel in the glittering surf of conquest like a joyous bather in a sunny sea. But it was only a partial victory. The apparent capitulation of the upper and middle classes was illusory, and even the man in the street who heard about him and wondered was moved by an uneasy suspicion that all was not well. For, in spite of the flattery and the amusement, Oscar Wilde never succeeded in winning popular respect. His intellectual playfulness destroyed popular faith in his sincerity, and the British people have still to learn that one can be as serious in one's play with ideas as in one's play with a football. The danger of his position was all the more serious because those who were ready to laugh with him were never tired of laughing at him. This showed that lack of confidence which is the most fertile ground of suspicion, and Wilde was always suspected in this country even before the rumours which culminated in his trial and imprisonment began to filter through the higher strata of society to the lower. It sufficed that he was strange and clever and seemingly happy and indifferent to public opinion. This popular suspicion is summarised clearly, and with the sort of disrespect from which he never escaped even in his hour of triumph, in an article in *Pearson's Weekly* for 27th May 1893, written immediately after the success of Lady Windermere's Fan and *A Woman of No Importance*:

> Where he does excel is in affectation. His mode of life, his manner of speech, his dress, his views, his work, are all masses of affectation. Affectation has become a second nature to him, and it would probably now be utterly impossible for him to revert to the original Oscar that lies beneath it all. In fact, probably none of his friends have ever had an opportunity of finding out what manner of man the real Oscar is. . . . So long as he remains an amiable eccentricity and the producer of amusing trifles, however,

one cannot be seriously angry with him. So far, it has never occurred to any reasonable person to take him seriously, and the storms of ridicule to which he has exposed himself have prevented his becoming a real nuisance. For the present, however, we may content ourselves with the reflection that there is no serious danger to be apprehended to the State from the vagaries of a butterfly.

The above may be taken as a fair example of the attitude of the popular Press towards Oscar Wilde, and the same sentiments were expressed, varying only in degrees of literary polish, in many directions, even at a time when the new spirit of comedy he had introduced into the British theatre was giving unbounded delight to a vast throng of fashionable playgoers; for these plays had not to create audiences for themselves, like the plays of Bernard Shaw; they were immediately acclaimed, and Wilde at once took rank with popular playwrights like Sidney Grundy and Pinero.

There were of course many who admired him; and he always inspired friendship among his intimates. All who have written of him during his earlier period and during the early days of his triumph refer to his joyous and resplendent personality, his fine scholarship, his splendid manners and conversational gifts, his good humour and his lavish generosity. André Gide gives us many glimpses of Wilde both before and after his downfall, one of which reveals him as table-talker;

> I had heard him talked about at Stephane Mallarmé's house, where he was described as a brilliant conversationalist, and I expressed a wish to know him, little hoping that I should ever do so. A happy chance, or rather a friend, gave me the opportunity, and to him I made known my desire. Wilde was invited to dinner. It was at a restaurant. We were a party of four, but three of us were content to listen. Wilde did not converse—he told tales. During the whole meal he hardly stopped. He spoke in a slow, musical tone, and his very voice was wonderful. He knew French almost perfectly, but pretended, now and then, to hesitate for a word to which he wanted to call our attention. He had scarcely any accent, at least only what it pleased him to affect when it might give a somewhat new or strange appearance to a word—for instance, he used purposely to pronounce *scepticisme* as skepticisme. The stories he told us without a break that evening were not of his best. Uncertain of his audience, he was testing us, for, in his wisdom, or perhaps in his folly, he never betrayed himself into saying

anything which he thought would not be to the taste of his hearers; so he doled out food to each according to his appetite. Those who expected nothing from him got nothing, or only a little light froth, and as at first he used to give himself up to the task of amusing, many of those who thought they knew him will have known him only as the amuser.

With the progress of his triumph as a successful playwright, his friends observed a coarsening of his appearance and character, and he lost his powers of conversation. Robert H. Sherard met him during the Christmas season of 1894 and described his appearance as bloated. His face seemed to have lost its spiritual beauty, and he was oozing with material prosperity. At this time serious rumours about his private life and habits became more persistent in both London and Paris, and countenance was lent to them by the publication of *The Green Carnation*, which, although making no direct charge, hinted at strange sins. Oscar Wilde knew that his conduct must lead to catastrophe, although many of his friends believed in his innocence to the end. André Gide met him in Algiers just before the catastrophe happened. Wilde explained that he was fleeing from art:

He spoke of returning to London, as a well-known peer was insulting him, challenging him, and taunting him with running away.

'But if you go back what will happen?' I asked him. 'Do you know the risk you are running?'

'It is best never to know,' he answered. 'My friends are extraordinary— they beg me to be careful. Careful? But how can I be careful? That would be a backward step. I must go on as far as possible. I cannot go much further. Something is bound to happen . . . something else.'

Here he broke off, and the next day he left for England.

Almost immediately after his arrival he brought an action for criminal libel against the Marquis of Queensberry and, upon losing the case, was arrested, and charged under the 11th Section of the Criminal Law Amendment Act, and sentenced to two years' penal servitude. During his imprisonment he wrote *De Profundis*, in the form of a long letter to his friend, Robert Ross, a part of which was published in book form in 1905, and after his release he wrote *The Ballad of Reading Gaol*, published, under a pseudonym, 'C.3.3.' (his prison number), by Leonard Smithers, and he contributed two letters on the conditions of prison life, 'The Cruelties of Prison Life,' and 'Don't Read this if you Want to be Happy To-day,' to *The Daily Chronicle* on 28th May 1897 and 24th March 1898. These were his last writings.

After leaving prison he lived for a while, under the assumed name of 'Sebastian Melmoth,' at the Hôtel de la Plage, and later at the Villa Bourget, Berneval-sur-Mer, near Dieppe, where he wrote *The Ballad of Reading Gaol*, and the prison letters, and where he contemplated writing a play called *Ahab and Jezebel*. This play he hoped would be his passport to the world again. But a new restlessness overcame him, and all his good resolutions turned to dust. For a while he travelled, visiting Italy, the south of France and Switzerland, eventually settling in Paris, where he died, in poverty and a penitent Catholic, on 30th November 1900. He was buried in the Bagneux Cemetery, but on 20th July 1909 his remains were removed to Père Lachaise.

It is too soon, perhaps, even now, to set a final value upon the work of Oscar Wilde. Time although not an infallible critic, is already winnowing the chaff from the grain, and almost with the passing of each year we are better able to recognise the more permanent essences of his literary remains. It is inevitable in his case, where the glamour of personality added so significantly to the character of his work, that Time should insist upon being something more than a casual arbiter. In proof of this the recollection of so much futile criticism of Wilde cannot be overlooked. Both the man and his work have suffered depreciations which amount to defamation, and appraisals which can only be described as silly. But finally he would seem in many instances to have suffered more at the hands of his friends than his enemies. There have been, to be sure, several wise estimations of his genius, even in this country, notably those of Arthur Ransome and the not altogether unprovocative essays of Arthur Symons, entitled 'An Artist in Attitudes'; and the various prefaces and notes contributed by Robert Ross to certain of the volumes in the complete edition of the works are, of course, of great value. But, as the incidents associated with the life and times of Wilde recede further into the background of the mental picture which inevitably forms itself about any judgment of his work, we shall be able to obtain a less biased view. Even then, our perspective may be wrong, for this difficulty of personality is not only dominant, but it may be essential.

The personality of Oscar Wilde, luxuriant, piquant and insolent as it was, is sufficiently emphatic to compel attention so long as interest in his ideas or his works survives. Indeed, it may never be quite possible to separate such a man from such work. It is certainly impossible to do so now. With many writers, perhaps the majority, it requires no effort to forget the author in the book, because literature has effectually absorbed personality, or all that was distinctive of the author's personality. With Oscar Wilde it is otherwise. His books can never be the abstract and brief chronicles of himself; for, admittedly on his part, and recognisably on the part of others, he put even more distinction into his life than he did into his art. Not always the worthier part of himself; for that often, and more often in his last phase, was reserved for his books. But there is little doubt that the complete Oscar Wilde was the living and bewildering personality which rounded itself off and blotted itself out in a tragedy which was all the more nihilistic because of its abortive attempt at recuperation—an attempt which immortalised itself in the repentant sincerity of *De Profundis*, but almost immediately fell forward into an anticlimax of tragedy more pitiful than the first.

So far as we are able to judge, and with the aid of winnowing Time, it is already possible to single out the small contribution made by Oscar Wilde to poetry. The bulk of his poetry is negligible. It represents little more than the ardent outpourings of a young man still deeply indebted to his masters. One or two lyrics will of a surety survive in the anthologies of the future, but if Wilde were dependent upon his verses for future acceptance his place would be among the minor poets. There is, however, a reservation to be made even here, as there is in almost every generalisation about this elusive personality; he wrote three poems, two towards the close of his earlier period, *The Harlot's House* and *The Sphinx*, and one near the close of his life, The Ballad of *Reading Gaol*, which bear every indication of permanence. The two former will appeal to those who respond to strange and exotic emotions, the other to those who are moved by the broader current of average human feeling. His last poem, and last work, does not reveal merely Oscar Wilde's acceptance of a realistic attitude, it reveals what might have been, had he lived to pursue the matter further, conversion to a natural and human acceptation of life. The sense of simplicity in art which previously he had been content to use as a refuge for the consciously complex, as a sort of intensive culture for modern bewilderment, is now used with even greater effect in the cause of the most obvious of human emotions—pity:

I never saw a man who looked
With such a wistful eye
Upon that little tent of blue
Which prisoners call the sky,
And at every drifting cloud that went
With sails of silver by.

I walked, with other souls in pain,
Within another ring,
And was wondering if the man had done

A great or little thing,
When a voice behind me whispered low,
'*That fellow's got to swing*'

There is none of the old earnest insincerity in this poem, and only
occasionally does the poet fall back into the old *bizarrerie*. Had *The Ballad of
Reading Goal* been written a hundred years ago, it would have been printed as
a broadside and sold in the streets by the balladmongers; it is so common as
that, and so great as that. But there is nothing common, and nothing great, in
the universal sense, about the two earlier poems. These are distinguished only
as the expressions of unusual vision and unusual mood; they are decadent in
so far as they express emotions that are sterile and perverse. They are decadent
in the sense that Baudelaire was decadent, from whom they inherit almost
everything save the English in which they are framed. But few will doubt
their claim to a place in a curious artistic niche. *The Sphinx*, a masterly fantasy
of bemused artificiality, is really a poetic design, an arabesque depending for
effect upon hidden rhymes and upon strange fancies, expressing sensations
which have hitherto been enshrined in art rather than in life:

> Your eyes are like fantastic moons that shiver in some stagnant lake,
> Your tongue is like some scarlet snake that dances to fantastic tunes,
> Your pulse makes poisonous melodies, and your black throat is like the
>   hole
> Left by some torch or burning coal on Saracenic tapestries.

Similarly, 'The Harlot's House' interprets a mood that is so sinister and
impish and unusual as to express disease rather than health:

> Sometimes a horrible marionette
> Came out, and smoked its cigarette
> Upon the steps like a live thing.
> Then turning to my love, I said,
> 'The dead are dancing with the dead,
> The dust is whirling with the dust.'
> But she—she heard the violin,
> And left my side, and entered in:
> Love passed into the house of lust.

Wilde developed this abnormal attitude towards life in *The Picture of
Dorian Gray* and in *Salomé,* and in each of these prose works he endeavours,
often with success, to stimulate feelings that are usually suppressed, by means

of what is strange and rare in art and luxury. It is not the plot that you think about whilst reading *Salomé*, but the hidden desire of the author to tune the senses and the mind to a preposterous key:

"I have jewels hidden in this place—jewels that thy mother even has never seen; jewels that are marvellous to look at. I have a collar of pearls, set in four rows. They are like unto moons chained with rays of silver. They are even as half a hundred moons caught in a golden net. On the ivory breast of a queen they have rested. Thou shalt be as fair as a queen when thou wearest them.

I have amethysts of two kinds; one that is black like wine, and one that is red like wine that one has coloured with water. I have topazes yellow as are the eyes of tigers, and topazes that are pink as the eyes of a wood-pigeon, and green topazes that are as the eyes of cats. I have opals that burn always, with a flame that is cold as ice, opals that make sad men's minds, and are afraid of the shadows. I have onyxes like the eyeballs of a dead woman. I have moonstones that change when the moon changes, and are wan when they see the sun. I have sapphires big like eggs, and as blue as blue flowers. The sea wanders within them, and the moon comes never to trouble the blue of their waves. I have chrysolites and beryls, and chrysoprases and rubies; I have sardonyx and hyacinth stones, and stones of chalcedony, and I will give them all unto thee, all, and other things will I add to them.

The King of the Indies has but even now sent me four fans fashioned from the feathers of parrots, and the King of Numidia a garment of ostrich feathers. I have a crystal, into which it is not lawful for a woman to look, nor may young men behold it until they have been beaten with rods. In a coffer of nacre I have three wondrous turquoises. He who wears them on his forehead can imagine things which are not, and he who carries them in his hand can turn the fruitful woman into a woman that is barren.

These are great treasures. They are treasures above all price. But this is not all. In an ebony coffer I have two cups of amber that are like apples of pure gold. If an enemy pour poison into these cups they become like apples of silver. In a coffer incrusted with amber I have sandals incrusted with glass. I have mantles that have been brought from the land of the Serer, and bracelets decked about with carbuncles and with jade that come from the city of Euphrates. . . .

What desirest thou more than this, Salomé? Tell me the thing that thou desirest, and I will give it thee. All that thou askest I will give thee, save one thing only. I will give thee all that is mine, save only the life of one man. I will give thee the mantle of the high priest. I will give thee the veil of the sanctuary."

The mere naming of jewels and treasures in a highly wrought prose-poem might in itself be as innocent as one of Walt Whitman's catalogues of implements, but even removed from its context there is something unusual and even sinister about Herod's offering to Salomé. The whole work is coloured by a hunger for sensation that is negative with excess of civilisation.

In the essays collected under the title *Intentions,* Oscar Wilde has let us into the secret which produced these works. That secret is involved in an attempt to push Gautier's idea of art for art's sake, and Whistler's idea of art as Nature's exemplar, to their logical conclusions. He outdoes his masters with the obvious intention of going one better. Throughout the whole of his life he was filled with a boyish enthusiasm which took the form of self-delight. 'His attitude was dramatic,' says Arthur Symons, 'and the whole man was not so much a personality as an attitude. Without being a sage, he maintained the attitude of a sage; without being a poet, he maintained the attitude of a poet; without being an artist he maintained the attitude of an artist.' It is certainly true that his intellect was dramatic, and it is equally true that he was fond of adopting attitudes, but it is far from true to name three of his favourite attitudes and to say that these began and ended in the mere posture. For Oscar Wilde was both poet and sage and artist. He may not have been a great poet, he may not have been a great sage, he may not, which is more doubtful, have been a great artist, but the fact remains that the attitudes representing those faculties and adopted by him, were the symbols of demonstrable phases of his genius. Whilst always longing to express himself in literary forms, and knowing himself to be capable of doing so, he found it easier to express himself through the living personality. Writing bored him, and those who knew him are agreed that he did not put the best of himself into his work. 'It is personalities,' he said, 'not principles, that move the age.'

Throughout the whole of his life he tried to live up, not to his blue-and-white china, but to an idea of personality; and the whole of his philosophy is concerned with an attempt to prove that personality, even though it destroy itself, should be the final work of art. Indeed, in his opinion, art itself was nothing but the medium of personality. His attitudes thus become details in the art of personality. If they had no basis in fact, Oscar Wilde would have been no more than an actor playing a part in a work of art, but although he played, played at intellectual dandy, much as a boy will play at pirates, he was playing a part in the drama of life; and he adopted the attitude of dandy in response to as real an emotion at least as that which inspires a boy to adopt the attitude of pirate. What he seemed to be doing all the time was translating life into art through himself. His books were but incidents in this process. He always valued life more than art, and only appreciated the latter when its reflex action contributed something to his sensations; but because he had thought himself into the position of one who transmutes life into art, he fell into the error of imagining art to be more important than life. And art for him was not only those formal and plastic things which we call the fine arts; it embraced all luxurious artificialities. 'All art is quite useless,' he said. Such an attitude was in itself artificial; but with Oscar Wilde this artificialism lacked any progressive element: it was sufficient in itself; in short, it ended in itself, and not in any addition to personal power. Oscar Wilde never, for instance, dreamt of evolving into a god; he dreamt of evolving into a master of sensation, a harp responding luxuriously to every impression. This he became, or rather, this he always was, and it explained the many quite consistent charges of plagiarism that were always being brought against him, and it may explain his insensate plunge into forbidden sin, his conversion and his relapse. He lived for the mood, but whatever that mood brought him, whether it was the ideas of others or the perversities of what is impish in life, he made them his own. What he stole from Whistler, Pater, Balzac, Gautier and Baudelaire, whilst remaining recognisably derivative, had added unto them something which their originals did not possess. He mixed pure wines, as it were, and created a new complex beverage, not perhaps for quaffing, but rather a liqueur, with a piquant and quite original flavour which still acknowledged the flavours of its constituents.

This, then, was in reality an attitude towards life, and not an empty pose. I do not think that Oscar Wilde had any hope of finding anything absolute; he was born far too late in the nineteenth century for that. He had no purpose in life save play. He was the playboy of the Nineties; and, like the hero of John Millington Synge's drama, he was subject to the intimidation of flattery. Naturally inclined to go one better than his master, he was also inclined to please his admirers and astonish his enemies by going one better than himself, and as this one better generally meant in his later life one more extravagance, one further abandonment, it resulted, from the point of view of convention, in his going always one worse. Repetition of this whim turned perversity into a habit, and the growing taunt of those who knew or suspected his serious perversions drove him into the final perversion of deliberately courting tragedy, much as the mouse is charmed back into the clutches of the cat after it has apparently been given a loophole of retreat. It would not have been cowardice if Oscar Wilde had escaped while he had the chance, and it was not bravery that made him blind to that chance; he was bemused by his own attitude. Afterwards, he learnt the meaning of pain, and he arrived at a conclusion similar to that of Nietzsche. But it was not until afterwards. And although he found consolation in Christian mysticism whilst in prison, and again on his deathbed, we shall never know with what subtle joy he permitted his own destruction during the intervening period. Looked at from such a point of view, his books help in explaining the man. The best of them, *Intentions, The House of Pomegranates, The Importance of Being Earnest, The Soul of Man, The Ballad of Reading Gaol, De Profundis,* and a handful of epigrams and short parables which he called *Prose Poems,* must, it seems to me, take a definite place in English literature as the expression and explanation of the type Wilde represented.

This type was not created by Oscar Wilde: it was very general throughout Europe at the close of the last century, and he represented only one version of it. Probably to himself he imagined himself to approximate somewhat to the cynical idlers of his plays: Lord Goring in *An Ideal Husband,* Lord Darlington in *Lady Windermere's Fan,* Lord Illingworth in *A Woman of No Importance* and Algernon Moncrieff in *The Importance of Being Earnest* may be partial portraits of the sort of personal impression their author imagined he was creating in the fashionable world. But he drew fuller portraits of himself in his novel. Lord Henry Wotton and Dorian Gray represent two sides of Oscar Wilde; they are both experimenters in life, both epicureans and both seeking salvation by testing life to destruction. *The Picture of Dorian Gray* is really a moral tale, and that also is characteristic of the genius of Oscar Wilde, for at no period of his life had he the courage of his amorality. He was always haunted by the still small voice which broke bounds and expressed itself freely in *De Profundis.* And whilst reading his books, or listening to his plays, one cannot help feeling that their very playfulness is but the cloak of tragedy. The decadent, weary with known joys and yearning for new sensations, perpetually being rebuked by the clammy hand of exhausted desire, must needs laugh. Oscar Wilde laughed, and made us laugh, not by his wit so much as by his humour, that humour which dances over his plays and epigrams with the flutter of sheet lightning, compelling response where response is possible, but always inconsequent and always defying analysis. It reached its height in *The Importance of Being*

Earnest, a comedy so novel, so irresistibly amusing and so perfect in its way that discussion of it ends in futility, like an attempt to explain the bouquet of old Cognac or the iridescence of opals. It is the moonshine of genius. The still small voice in him, of which his lambent humour is the mask, lurks also in 'The Soul of Man' and *The Ballad of Reading Gaol*, and it is quite possible that had he lived the even life that he began to live on the bleak coast of Normandy after his release from prison, this underlying strain in his character would have turned him into a social reformer. His harrowing letters on prison conditions point to that when associated with his philosophic dash into the realm of Socialism. As it was, such humanitarian zeal as he had ended on the one side in pity and on the other in the dream of a Utopia for dandies.

Dandy of intellect, dandy of manners, dandy of dress, Oscar Wilde strutted through the first half of the Nineties and staggered through the last. So pleased was he with himself, so interested was he in the pageant of life, that he devoted his genius, in so far as it could be public, to telling people all about it. His genius expressed itself best in stories and conversation, and he was always the centre of each. The best things in his plays are the conversations, the flippancies of dandies and the garrulities of delightful shameless dowagers. His best essays are colloquies; those that are not depend for effect upon epigrams and aphorisms, originally dropped by himself in the dining-rooms and *salons* of London and Paris. When he was not conversing he was telling stories, and these stories perhaps, the *Prose Poems*, *The House of Pomegranates* and *The Happy Prince*, will outlive even his wittiest paradox. *Salomé* is more a story, a 'prose-poem,' than a play, and it is more, to use for once the method of inversion in which he delighted, an epigram than a story. One can imagine the glee with which Oscar Wilde worked up to the anti-climax, to the moment after Salomé has kissed the dead mouth of Jokanaan, and Herod has turned round and said: 'Kill that woman.' One can taste his own delight whilst writing the final stage instruction: 'The soldiers run forward and crush beneath their shields Salomé, daughter of Herodias, Princess of Judaea.' But more easily still can one imagine this remarkable man for ever telling himself an eternal tale in which he himself is hero.

—Holbrook Jackson, "Oscar Wilde:
The Last Phase," chapter iv of
The Eighteen Nineties, 1913, pp. 72–90

Edward Shanks "Oscar Wilde" (1924)

Edward Shanks was a playwright, journalist, and editor who, in this extract, examines the reception of Wilde beyond his Anglo-American audience and among his generally more admiring and sympathetic readers on the Continent. By the time Shanks writes in 1924, he states that few critics or readers in England would judge Wilde to be anything more than a second-rate writer, and yet in Germany, for example, he is classed alongside Shakespeare as a writer gifted by England to the world (readers should be unsurprised that critics such as Shanks, who incorporated Wilde into an English rather than Irish canon, had been making Irish writers such as Yeats and Joyce irate for years, as those two writers' reviews in this volume show).

These Continental attitudes to Wilde force Shanks to question the contemporary British conception of the author, and, as a consequence, he attempts to contextualize Wilde among other English writers of the mid- and late Victorian periods, examining whether Wilde's art stands up in quality beside those other artists. The extract details critical assumptions typical of the modernist period, and readers might note that Shanks several times refers to his period's undergraduates' literary interests and how, if once Wilde was a favorite among university youth, he was no longer.

Ultimately, Shanks sees Wilde as more likely to be remembered for his personal history rather than as an artist. He views Wilde's literary output as being derivative without mentioning Wilde's artistic use of the material he borrowed. Contemporary critics have begun to focus more on the manner in which Wilde took from fellow artists and transformed their work into something distinctly his own. Shanks sees little suggestion of any artistic use of other material in Wilde's art, only a succession of plagiarisms. The conclusion makes some rich statements about the Decadent movement in the 1890s in England, Wilde's role therein, and the popular antipathy he aroused both as a symbol for that movement and as one of its mainstays. From a position of critical and historical distance, Shanks was able to speak of decadence as a "movement" in a manner in which critics of only a few years earlier would have been incapable. These sorts of literary critical creations, of movements and aesthetic preferences, are well evidenced in this extract.

A little while ago, by way of celebrating the centenary of Byron's death, nearly every critic in England felt himself in honour bound to attempt to explain why that poet holds a higher place in Continental, than in English, estimation. It is a matter that has been canvassed again and again, and in the course of innumerable discussions some light, I think, has been thrown on the problem, which is one of the prettiest in all the theory of international literature. Byron was a great, and above all a typical figure: he did not so much invent Byronism as give it a name, and that because he was the first to isolate it in large and recognisable quantities from the confused emotional material of the age. His career was spectacular, and his end both spectacular and heroic. Moreover, what now makes us rank him somewhat lower than do Continental readers is something which is more apparent to us than to them, something which hides more from us than from them his none the less real virtues. The intolerable roughness and even shoddiness of his style are facts which do, for us, fight against his strength and originality: for foreigners, reading him whether in translation or in the original, they are necessarily facts of less weight.

Now the position of Oscar Wilde, here and abroad, has many points of similarity to this. We tend here more and more to look on him as a writer decidedly of the second rate. His influence, never very strong with the mature, grows less and less even with the young; and undergraduates are ceasing to quote his epigrams in their essays. The time is perhaps coming when it will no longer be a hopeful enterprise to revive his plays. It would not be easy to find any critic of literature who would be likely to refer to him as a considerable writer. Nevertheless, even with us, his name conveys a vague sense as of something important, and abroad it does much more than that. In Germany, certainly, most critics would name Shakespeare, Byron and Wilde as the three writers whom England has given to the world.

Those who say this may make themselves seem a little absurd to us; but what they state is a fact and not an opinion. In literature the persons whom a nation gives to the world are those whom the world consents to accept from her. We may continue to offer Shelley, Keats and Wordsworth as alternatives, but it is Byron that is chosen. We may offer as an alternative either George Meredith or Mr. Hardy, if we please, but it is Wilde that is chosen. This is a fact and, instead of looking at it as though it were an inexplicable curiosity of nature, we shall do well to ask ourselves whether it does not spring from a fact of even greater interest, whether we must not in view of it apply to Wilde standards rather different from those applicable to writers who are ours alone, whether we should not attempt to see in him something more than simply an author of English prose and verse.

At first sight, the parallel with Byron does not appear likely to be very fruitful. Byron's virtues, we have said, are to some extent obscured from us by the roughness of his style. But, though Wilde may not have been—and I do not think that it can be maintained that he was—in the first rank of English prose-writers, yet smoothness, brilliance and glitter of style are among the chief of his qualities. For the rest, a certain similarity of fate is obvious enough; but Wilde's downfall and his wretched death in Paris make but a sordid caricature of Byron's mysterious exile from England and his heroic death in Greece.

When we consider Wilde, of course, the imagination is stirred by that sudden and disastrous reversal of fortune, by fate's evident rebuke to good luck too great and too insolently borne. He set out at an early period to make himself, with apparently small materials, a conspicuous figure, and when he fell, it was, for apparently small reason, in a blaze of conspicuousness. But such things do not happen quite accidentally, and their causes must be sought.

Let us, once and for all, be frank about his offence. It was a squalid and disgusting business, with every circumstance of vulgarity and some of madness. But the crime for which he was sentenced was not a great crime. It was one which goes oftener known and unpunished than any other; and Wilde was not a great sinner, no Nero or Heliogabalus or Caesar Borgia.

Yet he and the public at large were for the first time at one in holding that he was a great sinner. The crowds which howled savagely outside the Old Bailey after he had been found guilty, he himself writing *De Profundis* in Reading Gaol agreed that he was an enemy of society whom society had crushed. He says:

> Of course I know that from one point of view things will be made different for me than for others; must indeed, by the very nature of the case, be made so. The poor thieves and outcasts who are imprisoned here with me are in many respects more fortunate than I am. The little way in grey city or green field that saw their sin is small; to find those who know nothing of what they have done they need go no further than a bird might fly between the twilight and the dawn; but for me the world is shrivelled to a handsbreadth, and everywhere I turn my name is written on the rocks in lead. For I have come, not from obscurity into the momentary notoriety of time, but from a sort of eternity of fame to a sort of eternity of infamy, and sometimes seem to myself to have shown, if indeed it

required showing, that between the famous and the infamous there is but one step, if as much as one.

There is in this much of the megalomania which undoubtedly was one of the causes contributory to his disaster. It makes a peculiar contrast with the picture of Wilde, after his release, loafing outside the Café de la Paix, to invite the recognition and the curiosity and the free drinks of chance English tourists, one of whom, questioned as to whether anything had struck him about Wilde, replied: 'Yes, he always wore tartan mittens.' But in what I have quoted there is something more than megalomania. At the time, Wilde's fall reverberated hugely and the echoes of it have not really yet died away. He had, to be sure, enjoyed a very great reputation, as literary reputations go; but it is not often that an English man of letters secures, by whatever means, such a place in the public imagination as this. The thing becomes more peculiar when we repeat that he was not a writer of the first rank or even of marked originality. This is, in short, the problem to be examined.

His first book of importance, the *Poems* of 1881, is in its way a peculiar collection. It is evidently the work of a man of much talent; but it is exceedingly like a volume of serious parodies. Young poets imitate, they cannot as a rule help imitating, what they have admired. This is part of the stage of immaturity and does no harm. But one's first impression on reading these early pieces by Wilde is that a young man who could imitate so fluently, so copiously and so successfully the manners of so many different masters ought to be engaged in original work. He copies even Milton whom, however, he sees through a mist, as it were, of Wordsworth. This is the opening of his sonnet on the Bulgarian atrocities:

Christ, dost them live indeed? or are thy bones
Still straitened in their rock-hewn sepulchre?
And was thy Rising only dreamed by her
Whose love of thee for all her sin atones?
For here the air is horrid with men's groans,
The priests who call upon thy name are slain,
Dost thou not hear the bitter wail of pain
From those whose children lie upon the stones?

The very excellence of the thing—for of its kind it is excellent—almost takes one's breath away. As one goes on one finds more that is surprising. The combined manners of Keats, Morris and Swinburne come in very usefully to help a young man, who has absolutely nothing of his own to say, to three ornate narrative poems. There are ballads reminiscent of Swinburne and Rossetti. Andrew Lang's attempt to found an English Pléiade echoes here in a villanelle on Theocritus—of all poets in the world! Contemporaries in France have their share with "Impression du Matin" and other pieces. Tennyson too is laid under contribution; and the best and simplest of the shorter poems is actually an echo of Tom Hood.

In the ordinary way there would be more malevolence than usefulness in such an analysis as this of the work of a young writer. But in the ordinary way the young writer, so long as he is thus copying his favourite models, is still plainly learning his job. By the time he has learnt how to imitate Swinburne or Keats, or whomever it may be, smoothly and successfully, he has ceased to wish to do anything of the kind. But for Wilde the styles of other poets were part of his material; and he sometimes appropriates them with so persuasive an air of having the right to do it, that one is left at a loss to say whether the results are truly independent and his own or not.

In the shorter poems, this peculiarity is of little importance, for the poems themselves are of practically none. Wilde's reputation as a poet rests almost entirely on two pieces, both of which are derivative in style and yet both of which have a life of their own. *The Sphinx* gives its author's age as under twenty, which, to speak with frankness, I cannot bring myself to believe. It is much too remarkable an exercise in literary decoration for this to be possible, when one compares it with the other work of the same kind.

It is remarkable, and it *is* an exercise. But for Baudelaire and Swinburne it could never have been written. Cato and the fascination of sin, the names of precious stones and other 'stunning' words, as Rossetti called them, a sinister disillusionment with life and hints at strange vices—it is hard to say what in this is the contribution of the poet. Perhaps the form: for the stanza of *In Memoriam* undergoes a definite and interesting change when it is written as a couplet, with the rhymes concealed and not dwelt on. It takes on a different movement, very characteristic and rather impressive. This is, I fancy, Wilde's one invention in literary technique.

But so much will not explain the definite impression made on us that the poem is a valid work of art, and not to be dismissed as derivative or insincere, though both these faults could be shown in it. But what is to be made of such a passage as this?

Or had you shameful secret guests and did you hurry to your home
Some Nereid coiled in amber foam with curious rock crystal breasts?

Or did you treading through the froth call to the brown Sidonian
For tidings of Leviathan, Leviathan or Behemoth?

Or did you when the sun was set climb up the cactus-covered slope
To meet your swarthy Ethiop whose body was of polished jet?

Or did you while the earthen skiffs dropped down the grey nilotic flats
At twilight and the flickering bats flew round the temple's triple glyphs

Steal to the border of the bar and swim across the silent lake
And slink into the vault and make the Pyramid your lupanar

Till from each black sarcophagus rose up the painted swathed dead?
Or did you lure unto your bed the ivory-horned Tragelaphos?

When the undergraduate (or so, at least, it used to be) reads this for the first time his heart leaps up, for he beholds what an immense amount of entertainment can be got of mere words. And one's instinct still is to say of *The Sphinx*: This is great fun! For it is entirely something, and it is equally certainly nothing on a higher level than that. The extravagance of the decoration is at once self-conscious and naïve. The ideas are mere counters, and the poem expresses no feeling, unless it be a delight in verbal and metrical virtuosity. But as such it exists and has an enduring spark of life in it.

The Ballad of Reading Gaol is a different matter. It was written later in Wilde's life, it describes an actual experience, and it is meant to convey a real feeling. But it too is derivative and its derivations are curious. One can understand that Wilde should again have taken something from Tom Hood for this purpose, but his borrowing from Coleridge is a good deal less easy to explain. Yet it is undoubtedly there:

They glided past, they glided fast,
Like travellers through a mist:
They mocked the moon in a rigadoon
Of delicate turn and twist.
And with formal pace and loathsome grace
The phantoms kept their tryst.

With mop and mow, we saw them go,
Slim shadows hand in hand:
About, about, in ghostly rout
They trod a saraband:
And the damned grotesques made arabesques,
Like the wind upon the sand!

This is as self-conscious in its decorative effect as are the passages in which Wilde remembers suddenly and too clearly that he is describing a realistic modern tragedy:

> The Governor was strong upon
> The Regulations Act:
> The Doctor said that Death was but
> A scientific fact:
> And twice a day the Chaplain called,
> And left a little tract.

How are we to reconcile these incongruities and the constant straining of feeling throughout the poem, as in the verses beginning 'Yet each man kills the thing he loves,' with the evident fact that it is a work of power and beauty? Yet it makes a deep impression on almost all who read it, and very much the impression that Wilde intended, of a compassionate revolt against the cruelty of human justice. We can only say that a certain kind of insincerity was natural and essential in Wilde and, for the moment, leave it at that.

The reaching after effect which is the prime force of *The Sphinx* and the disfigurement of *The Ballad of Reading Gaol* is less disconcerting in his prose than in his verse. In prose it can, and very often does, take the form of wit, whereas in verse it takes too often the form of false emotion. And, in so far as Wilde's fame is based on his works at all, it is based on four or five works in prose, on *The Importance of Being Earnest* and *Lady Windermere's Fan*, on *De Profundis* and *Intentions* and *A House of Pomegranates* and *The Picture of Dorian Gray*.

It is here, it seems to me, that his genius, as expressed in his writings, is most often exaggerated. His habit of epigram, which makes a restless glitter over the surface of his plays and stories, can be parallelled from the novels of Disraeli, from whom too he derives his quite conscious and not all fatuous delight in aristocracy and opulence. Some of his sayings are acute and some are shallow; but, as the conversational epigrammatist will, he contrives to make them all look exactly alike.

> I adore simple pleasures. They are the last refuge of the complex.
> No nice girl should ever waltz with such particularly younger sons! It looks so fast!
> Better to take pleasure in a rose than to put its root under a microscope.
> Nothing is so dangerous as being too modern. One is apt to grow old-fashioned quite suddenly.

The prose of which such are the high lights is not of the first order, whether in style or in wisdom; and when he aims at beauty it cannot be said that he reaches a much higher level:

> But, see, it is dawn already. Draw back the curtains and open the windows wide. How cool the morning air is! Piccadilly lies at our feet like a long riband of silver. A faint purple mist hangs over the Park, and the shadows of the white houses are purple. It is too late to sleep. Let us go down to Covent Garden and look at the roses. Come! I am tired of thought.

Let us then turn to the stories. The fairy-stories are charming; but will it be seriously maintained that they or *Lord Arthur Savile's Crime* are works of a high order? The stories in this second book are excellently ingenious and would be popular at any time and in almost any hands, but they are slight. A trivial thing may be a great work of art, if it displays a passionate delight in triviality; but these do not. And *The Picture of Dorian Gray* is disappointingly little more than ingenious. The idea is magnificent, even if it is a little too bizarre to be the vehicle for very intense feeling. The 'Preface' is almost portentous, the most challenging and sweeping statement of the theory of art for art's sake ever made. But Wilde has sacrificed what might have been a masterpiece to his desire for immediate effect. Tussore silk curtains, opium-scented cigarettes, dressing-tables with large gold-topped bottles on them—these are the unhappy symbols, the first that came to hand, which Wilde employed for the embodiment of what after all was a vision of beauty. There is a book similar in spirit, by one of Wilde's favourite authors, which affords a fair comparison. It is verbose and ill-constructed, but it does to perfection what *Dorian Gray* fails to do. It is *Mademoiselle de Maupin*; and the comparison is fatal to Wilde.

We proceed to the plays, his most successful works. These were written frankly for money; but they are none the worse for that. Of their kind indeed they are very good. All his life he had treated the world as a theatre, and it required no great effort for him to submit himself to theatrical requirements. His stage effects are carried out with a gusto and sweep that make them exhilarating. Look at the curtain for the first act of *Lady Windermere's Fan*:

LADY WINDERMERE
Arthur, if that woman comes here—I warn you—

LORD WINDERMERE
Margaret, you'll ruin us!

LADY WINDERMERE
Us! from this moment my life is separate from yours. But if you wish to avoid a public scandal, write at once to this woman and tell I forbid her to come here!

LORD WINDERMERE
I will not—I cannot—she must come!

LADY WINDERMERE
Then I shall do exactly as I have said. [Goes R.] You leave me no choice. [Exit R.]

LORD WINDERMERE
[Calling after her]. Margaret! Margaret! [A pause.] My God! What shall I do? I dare not tell her who this woman really is. The shame would kill her. [Sinks down into a chair and buries his face in his hands.]

One asks oneself involuntarily whether Wilde here has his tongue in his cheek or not. The scene is theatrical in the last degree, but effectively, magnificently theatrical. And the same may be said of the dialogue which was the element distinguishing his from the other 'well made' plays of the time. His dialogue of its sort is very fine and, considering that it exists only for its own sake, it is introduced very deftly so as not to give any impression that it retards the action of the play. But it is not dramatic prose of the highest order. It stands to Congreve's prose, for example, just as the scene I have quoted stands to the knocking at the gate in Macbeth.

Wilde's plays, if the distinction be permissible, have theatrical rather than dramatic qualities. They exist for effect, not for expression—all, that is to say, except one of them, *The Importance of Being Earnest*. This admirable piece does express something of the author and something which one would hardly have expected to find in him—a simple and light-hearted sense of fun.

It is more genuine than the other plays, and will probably outlive them all.

From this analysis, I have omitted *Salomé*, which is, perhaps, taking the whole world together, Wilde's most famous work, a fact not wholly due to Dr. Strauss's use of it as a libretto. It ranks, I think, somewhere with *The Sphinx* and with *Dorian Gray*. The idea is magnificently unexpected; but the execution is only superficial. From the elements of sin and blasphemy which it contains Wilde has made a very striking stage-picture but he had done no more. It is, however, a very characteristic work.

From this brief and rapid examination, I emerge with the verdict that Wilde was a derivative and artificial writer. He aimed constantly at effect rather than at expressing something genuine in himself. He took always the shortest and easiest way to an effect. Not one of his works but has in it the obvious seeds of decay. Yet the figure of Wilde survives; and it seems not unlikely that his legend will preserve some of his writings perhaps beyond their natural span of life.

The explanation is, I think, supplied by himself in *De Profundis*:

> I was a man who stood in symbolic relations to the art and culture of my age. I had realised this for myself at the very dawn of my manhood, and had forced my age to realise it afterwards. Few men hold such a position in their own lifetime, and have it so acknowledged. It is usually discerned, if discerned at all, by the historian, or the critic, long after both the man and his age have passed away. With me it was different. I felt it myself, and made others feel it. Byron was a symbolic figure, but his relations were to the passion of his age and its weariness of passion. Mine were to something more noble, more permanent, of more vital issue, of larger scope.

The parallel is unfortunate, for what Byron stood for was something decidedly stronger and more vital. But, like him, Wilde was a symbolic figure.

The origin of the movement he represented is not very easy to discover. It sprang perhaps from a revolt of part of the human race against a fate which seemed to be overtaking the whole. In the middle of the nineteenth century the wave of material improvement spread over the world and ugliness and narrowness came in its train. All the countries of Europe, one after another, were given up to industry, railways cut through their fields and the smoke of factory chimneys darkened their skies. Vast mean and degraded populations sprang up which had no songs nor any joy in life. The middle class, trading code of life ruled everywhere; and at once the artist sprang up in passionate reaction.

The reaction took different forms. Ruskin preached that pictures should have a religious effect on those who saw them. Morris, between his daydreams, laboured for the abandonment of machinery. Poets in France retired to ivory towers and ululated more or less distinctly from the top windows. And soon the rebels began to make themselves deliberately as unlike their enemies as they could. The middle classes applauded virtue, therefore vice was to be exalted. The middle classes preached thrift, therefore waste was to be practised. The middle classes thought art should be instructive, therefore all art was to be perfectly useless. And Baudelaire smoked opium and Verlaine alternated hysterically between religion and wickedness and Gérard de Nerval trailed a lobster after him through the streets of Paris.

The movement became extravagant and was doomed not to persist as it had begun, for it was approaching the evil in an unhelpful manner. But while it lasted it was a very real thing. And into it came Wilde, a young man not at all hysterical, with many talents and in particular a very great talent for histrionics. So he made himself the centre and symbol of all that great and bizarre crusade against bourgeois ideas and morality.

He was not an originator, he was, much as he would have disliked the designation, a populariser. He summarised in his work what was then called *fin de siècle* art, and made it easy for the great public to understand. Almost every aspect of the movement was there. The sensualism of Baudelaire and his hinting at strange vices, Gautier's disinterested immoral adoration of things, hard, bright and sharp-edged, Verlaine's religiosity—all these with dashes of Satanism and cruelty and just so much of the doctrines of Ruskin and Morris as could be made to fit in with the rest without too startling an incongruity. One might almost say that Wilde was not so much a writer as a museum.

It is not to be said that this view disposes of him either as a legend or as a writer; but it does, I think, explain him. He was artificial and insincere; but there was something genuine in his artificiality and something vital in his insincerity. These were his main qualities, and in both of them he was at heart consistent. He held up his mind as a mirror to a whole side of the life of his time, and in that mirror there may still be seen a wonderfully varied and interesting picture.

So, he having made himself the compendium of this movement, mankind treated him as its leader and turned and crushed him; and his name was removed from playbills and the crowds howled round the Old Bailey on learning that he had been sent to prison. He graciously gave the Decadence one head; and humanity with a brutal but sure instinct promptly cut it off. Life took the opportunity to affirm that art shall not be permitted to declare itself independent of life. For the reverse of his own parallel between himself and Byron is what is true. Byron, by whatever means, proclaimed the revolt of life, passionate, energetic, indignant life, against a world which was unworthy of it. The movement at the head of which Wilde, with incomparable but characteristic arrogance, placed himself, was, though I have called it a revolt, not so much that as an attempt at a secession. The Decadents did not contemplate the conquest of the world for better and nobler ideas. They stated their own superiority and contemptuously stepped aside. It was enough for them to make from time to time wounding remarks on the gross, struggling body of humanity which they had left behind them.

Now the Decadence was doomed to failure, whether it had received this wounding blow in the person of Wilde or not; and it does not rank very high among the movements which in the course of history have at one time and another swept over Europe. But it had in it some of the finest and acutest, if not some of the strongest, spirits of the time. Its achievement was incomplete, fragmentary, unhappy; but it achieved something. And a man who could make himself seem the typical figure of that movement and that achievement is not a man to be neglected.

Wilde, to be sure, deceived himself here as elsewhere. There was probably no really decadent strain in his nature. When, in *Dorian Gray*, he had to suggest abysmal wickedness he failed lamentably to make concrete the vague conception, and his attitude to the conception was all that could be desired from the severest of moralists. What distinguished him was the wax-like character of his mind which received a clear and readable impression of the main elements of his nature. This process of assimilation and simplification made him a leading figure and then a legend; and the legend, as I have said, will very likely make some of his works live longer than would otherwise be natural for them. But the man will always be more important than any of his works; and it will be a long time, I think, before he disappears altogether from memory.

—Edward Shanks, "Oscar Wilde,"
London Mercury, July 1924, pp. 278–287,
reprinted in *Second Essays on Literature*, 1927

❖

WORKS

❖

The following extracts examine various critics' views of particular works by Wilde, from his novel to his essays, his dramas to the letter and poem written after his downfall. In each, once more, the art of Wilde is inseparable from the critic's view of his character. Many of the following extracts explore Wilde's lack of "sincerity" as being either aesthetically necessary to his art or its major flaw. The question of the posing of the artist becomes of central importance when examining the two works published by Wilde after his conviction, *De Profundis* and "The Ballad of Reading Gaol," as each deals with questions of suffering, sin, and salvation. Is it possible to repent of one's past without regret for one's sin, as Wilde seems to claim? Is Wilde wholly to blame for his downfall or, as some extracts both in this section and earlier in the volume suggest, is it the English public whose misunderstanding and lack of appreciation are directly and shamefully responsible for Wilde's experience? Was Wilde more sinned against than sinning? Was he a sexual and/or an Irish martyr to English prejudice? Students can attempt to find answers to these questions in exploring the opinions presented from the following variety of perspectives.

The first two extracts are reviews of Wilde's sole novel, *The Picture of Dorian Gray*. The first is by the American essayist Julian Hawthorne, the second by Wilde's greatest aesthetic influence, Walter Pater. Hawthorne admires the originality of conception and the artistic audacity of the novel but believes, as other critics have also, that Dorian's portrait is a fuller "character" than the young man it portrays. Pater admires Wilde's art but questions the depiction of the interpretation of epicureanism (the philosophy that states that the pursuit of pleasure should be a human aim). The pleasure derived by readers of Wilde's volume of essays,

Intentions, is stated in the next two extracts to be primarily due to Wilde's sense of "play": his use of language and his playful dismissal of facts.

The next extract examines *A House of Pomegranates*, Wilde's second collection of what have been called "fairy stories." H.L. Menken admires the text and views it as Wilde's most distinguished aesthetic statement, but Menken also uses the review of Wilde's stories to launch a critique of the personality of their author and a broad and critical analysis of Wilde's aesthetic generally. The common critical elision of Wilde the man and Wilde the artist should be apparent to readers once more, but, unusually, Menken criticizes Wilde for not being *enough* of an aesthete and for having too much of the Puritan in his character as an artist.

The next eight extracts examine Wilde's dramatic works, although in regard to *Salomé* it should be remembered that, as the first two extracts correctly point out, it was not written to be performed on the stage. The two reviews of *Salomé* approach Wilde's play from different perspectives. The first is written by Alfred Douglas, Wilde's lover, and carries all Douglas's typical abuse for those critics who did not appreciate the play and for English society in general. The second, written by the American Edward Hale, Jr., does not particularly value the play itself but is useful to consult for its examination of the manner of Wilde's changeable personalities. The two extracts reviewing Wilde's play *A Woman of No Importance* are contrasts in the use to which critics employed reviews of particular works. The first is a detailed appreciation of the drama, its insights into life, its wit, and its use of language. The second is a platform for an attack on the English public's vilification of Wilde and an analysis of why such detestation of the artist and his work existed. The final four extracts dealing with Wilde's drama examine *The Importance of Being Earnest* and the structure of the play. The first extract by George Bernard Shaw, a playwright and theater critic who generally praised Wilde's dramas, in this instance criticizes the play for its mechanical structure and labored humor, viewing it as an old-fashioned farce similar to those written two decades earlier. The second extract, while stating Wilde's play is of unequalled quality, suggests that the third act suffers from having been written in the midst of increasing problems in Wilde's personal life. This extract also provides an example of the continuing public condemnation of Wilde several years after his imprisonment and the critiques of Wilde the author as inseparable from his art. The third extract examines the "marriage of form and manner" as evidenced in the play, suggesting that this was the genius of Wilde's staged "magic." The final extract, written in the 1920s, is evidence of how the play had become critically conceived by some as Wilde's masterpiece, a dramatic comedy unparalleled in English literature. John Drinkwater's remarks are not dissimilar to many of our own contemporary critical views of *The Importance of Being Earnest*.

The final three extracts explore Wilde's character as revealed by his letter, *De Profundis*, written from prison to Lord Alfred Douglas. Each suggests a different perspective on Wilde and the letter. The first sees in each another typically artistic pose; the second portrays Wilde as a Christlike martyr whose art can save society from its own sins; the third, in marked contrast to each of the two preceding abstracts, views Wilde's work after his downfall as evidence of his own sincere salvation, his "birth" through the suffering he had undergone in prison. With this final section, students should appreciate the continuing critical differences that exist in appreciations of Wilde as a man, as an artist, and as a criminal. It should also be apparent that, despite each review in this section discussing a particular literary work, Wilde's character and personality are inseparable in virtually all the critics' minds from the works themselves. If anything was a constant in Wilde's life and art, it was this lack of critical consistency in regard to his changing portrayals of himself.

THE PICTURE OF DORIAN GRAY

Julian Hawthorne
"The Romance of the Impossible" (1890)

Julian Hawthorne was an American essayist and reviewer, the son and the biographer of his father, the famous and popular author Nathaniel. This extract appeared in the same magazine that published the original serialized version of Wilde's story in 1890, a year before the expanded novel edition, and commends the story of Dorian Gray for its originality and its healthy departure from the ordinary. Even though Hawthorne admires Wilde's wit and skill with epigrams, he believes the characterization of the novel to be not fully developed: Lord Henry is favorably considered as a modern Mephistopheles and "Old Harry," or tempting devil, but the character of Dorian is critiqued as being much less developed in the novel than that of his own portrait. The fact that Hawthorne here reviews Wilde's novel in the same magazine that had published it should be taken into account by readers: Would a damning review have benefited the publisher or have continued the critical and public excitement that Wilde's novel had caused in London? Is all publicity good publicity? The conclusion of the review summarizing the plot of Wilde's story has not been included in this excerpt, but one might consider whether a boost in sales for *Lippincott's Monthly Magazine* was being considered when Hawthorne tantalized readers with the outline of the novel's strange plot.

Hawthorne seems to be largely admiring of the novel, but his contention that Dorian is only a partially realized character is still a comment heard today among critics of the text. He states that just as "nemo repente fuit turpissimus" (no one grows evil overnight), so equally as a first novelistic attempt, Wilde's text should be admired by readers. Perhaps, however, one might consider an actually admirable artistry in Dorian's lack of characterization: that Wilde intended to make the art of Dorian's portrait more real than the character of its subject. Readers might consider this lack of characterization as a deliberate and intelligent statement of Wilde's aesthetic philosophy: Art has a greater validity, is more real, than life itself.

Mr Oscar Wilde, the apostle of beauty, has in the July number of *Lippincott's Magazine* a novel or romance (it partakes of the qualities of both), which everybody will want to read. It is a story strange in conception, strong in interest, and fitted with a tragic and ghastly climax. Like many stories of its class, it is open to more than one interpretation; and there are, doubtless, critics who will deny that it has any meaning at all. It is, at all events, a salutary departure from the ordinary English novel, with the hero and heroine of different social stations, the predatory black sheep, the curate, the settlements, and Society. Mr Wilde, as we all know, is a gentleman of an original and audacious turn of mind, and the commonplace is scarcely possible to him. Besides, his advocacy of novel ideas in life, art, dress, and demeanour had led us to expect surprising things from him; and in this literary age it is agreed that a man may best show the best there is in him by writing a book. Those who read Mr Wilde's story in the hope of finding in it some compact and final statement of his theories of life and manners will be satisfied in some respects, and dissatisfied in others; but not many will deny that the book is a remarkable one, and would attract attention even had it appeared without the author's name on the title page.

The Picture of Dorian Gray begins to show its quality in the opening pages. Mr Wilde's writing has what is called 'colour,'—the quality that forms the mainstay of many of Ouïda's works,—and it appears in the sensuous descriptions of nature and of the decorations and environments of the artistic life. The general aspect of the characters and the tenor of their conversation remind one a little of *Vivian Gray* [sic] and a little of Pelham, but the resemblance does not go far: Mr Wilde's objects and philosophy are different from those of either Disraeli or Bulwer. Meanwhile his talent for aphorisms and epigrams may fairly be compared with theirs: some of his clever sayings are more than clever,—they show real insight and a comprehensive grasp. Their wit is generally cynical; but they are put into the mouth of one of the characters, Lord Harry, and Mr Wilde himself refrains from definitely committing himself to them; though one cannot help suspecting that Mr Wilde regards Lord Harry as being an uncommonly able fellow. Be that as it may, Lord Harry plays the part of Old Harry in the story, and lives to witness the destruction of every other person in it. He may be taken as an imaginative type of all that is most evil and most refined in modern civilisation,—a charming, gentle, witty, euphemistic Mephistopheles, who deprecates the vulgarity of goodness, and muses aloud about 'those renunciations that men have unwisely called virtue, and those natural rebellions that wise men still call sin.' Upon the whole, Lord Harry is the most ably portrayed character in the book, though not the most original in conception. Dorian Gray himself is as nearly a new idea in fiction as one has nowadays a right to expect. If he had been adequately realised and worked out, Mr Wilde's first novel would have been remembered after more meritorious ones were forgotten. But, even as 'nemo repente fuit turpissimus,' so no one, or hardly any one, creates a thoroughly original figure at a first essay. Dorian never quite solidifies. In fact, his portrait is rather the more real thing of the two.

—Julian Hawthorne, "The Romance of the Impossible," *Lippincott's Monthly Magazine*, September 1890, xlvi, pp. 412–415

WALTER PATER "A NOVEL BY MR. WILDE" (1891)

Walter Pater was an English essayist, stylist, aesthetician, novelist, and literary critic. He was a professor of classics at Oxford University when Wilde was an undergraduate and profoundly influenced the writers of the 1890s, Wilde not the least of all. When Pater published his 1873 *Studies in the History of the Renaissance*, the infamous conclusion of which encouraged the pursuit and enjoyment of "experience for its own sake," the young students and artists of the time took it to heart. Wilde called Pater's work his own "golden book" and suggested that "the last trump should have sounded" when it was written (the end of the world may as well have come). But Pater's work was immediately charged by critics with encouraging immorality, and he spent much of the following twenty years claiming to have been misinterpreted, rewriting his aesthetic philosophy in a more "socially responsible" manner.

Wilde's contemporary Frank Harris had claimed that Pater had refused to write a review of the novel when it first appeared in serialized form in *Lippincott's Monthly Magazine* in 1890, because it was "too dangerous." Considering what Pater had suffered critically over the years and that Wilde has written in the preface to his expanded 1891 novel that "There is no such thing as a moral or an immoral book," it is surprising that Pater agreed to review the text at all when it was published. But apart from finding Dorian an unsuccessful epicurean (a follower of the classical philosophy encouraging the pursuit of pleasure, variously interpreted at different times, as the chief human end), Pater was broadly admiring of *Dorian Gray*.

In the following review, Pater presents his own interpretation of epicureanism. He had published a novel himself, *Marius the Epicurean*, in 1885, which was considered to be a reworking of his earlier *Studies* and in which his philosophy took on a more wholesome, moral tone. There is certainly a sense that Pater is claiming here that Wilde misunderstood this form of the ancient philosophy, but Pater directs his criticisms only at the character of Dorian. He admires Wilde's artistry in handling and presenting the story, and recognizes various ways to approach it critically: as a supernatural tale, as a successful exercise in style, as a moral fable, and as a fictional presentation of aestheticism uninformed by the moral sense. For Pater, the suggestion at the conclusion of the extract that Wilde may have consciously imitated Poe and various French writers is no bar to valuing *Dorian Gray*. Pater no doubt recognized Wilde's rewriting of Pater's own *Studies* and *Marius*.

—⁓— —⁓— —⁓—

There is always something of an excellent talker about the writing of Mr. Oscar Wilde; and in his hands, as happens so rarely with those who practise it, the form of dialogue is justified by its being really alive. His genial, laughter-loving sense of life and its enjoyable intercourse, goes far to obviate any crudity there may be in the paradox, with which, as with the bright and shining truth which often underlies it, Mr. Wilde, startling his "countrymen," carries on, more perhaps than any other writer, the brilliant critical work of Matthew Arnold. "The Decay of Lying," for instance, is all but unique in its half-humorous, yet wholly convinced, presentment of certain valuable truths of criticism. Conversational ease, the fluidity of life, felicitous expression, are qualities which have a natural alliance to the successful writing of fiction; and side by side with Mr. Wilde's *Intentions* (so he entitles his critical efforts) comes a novel, certainly original, and affording the reader a fair opportunity of comparing his practise as a creative artist with many a precept he has enounced as critic concerning it.

A wholesome dislike of the common-place, rightly or wrongly identified by him with the *bourgeois,* with our middle-class—its habits and tastes—leads him to protest emphatically against so-called "realism" in art; life, as he argues, with much plausibility, as a matter of fact, when it is really awake, following art—the fashion an effective artist sets; while art, on the other hand, influential and effective art, has never taken its cue from actual life. In *Dorian Gray* he is true certainly, on the whole, to the aesthetic philosophy of his *Intentions;* yet not infallibly, even on this point: there is a certain amount of the intrusion of real life and its sordid aspects—the low theatre, the pleasures and griefs, the faces of some very unrefined people, managed, of course, cleverly enough. The interlude of Jim Vane, his half-sullen but wholly faithful care for his sister's honour, is as good as perhaps anything of the kind, marked by a homely but real pathos, sufficiently proving a versatility in the writer's talent, which should make his books popular. Clever always, this book, however, seems to set forth anything but a homely philosophy of life for the middle-class—a kind of dainty Epicurean theory, rather—yet fails, to some degree, in this; and one can see why. A true Epicureanism aims at a complete though harmonious development of man's entire organism. To lose the moral sense therefore, for instance, the sense of sin and righteousness, as Mr. Wilde's heroes are bent on doing as speedily, as completely as they can, is to lose, or lower, organisation, to become less complex, to pass from a higher to a lower degree of development. As a story, however, a partly supernatural story, it is first-rate in artistic management; those Epicurean niceties only adding to the decorative colour of its central figure, like so many exotic flowers, like the charming scenery and the perpetual, epigrammatic, surprising, yet so natural, conversations, like an atmosphere all about it. All that pleasant accessory detail, taken straight from culture, the intellectual and social interests, the conventionalities, of the moment, have, in fact, after all, the effect of the better sort of realism, throwing into relief the adroitly-devised supernatural element after the manner of Poe, but with a grace he never reached, which supersedes that earlier didactic purpose, and makes the quite sufficing interest of an excellent story. . . .

Dorian himself, though certainly a quite unsuccessful experiment in Epicureanism, in life as a fine art, is (till his inward spoiling takes visible effect suddenly, and in a moment, at the end of his story) a beautiful creation. But his story is also a vivid, though carefully considered, exposure of the corruption of a soul, with a very plain moral, pushed home, to the effect that vice and crime make people coarse and ugly. General readers, nevertheless, will probably care less for this moral, less for the fine, varied, largely appreciative culture of the writer, in evidence from page to page, than for the story itself, with its adroitly managed supernatural incidents, its almost equally wonderful applications of natural science; impossible, surely, in fact, but plausible enough in fiction. Its interest turns on that very old theme, old because based on some inherent experience or fancy of the human brain, of a double life: of Doppelganger—not of two *persons*, in this case, but of the man and his portrait; the latter of which, as we hinted above, changes, decays, is spoiled, while the former, through a long course of corruption, remains, to the outward eye, unchanged, still in all the beauty of a seemingly immaculate youth—"the devil's bargain." But it would be a pity to spoil the reader's enjoyment by further detail. We need only emphasise, once more, the skill, the real subtlety of art, the ease and fluidity withal of one telling a story by word of mouth, with which the consciousness of the supernatural is introduced into, and maintained amid, the elaborately conventional, sophisticated, disabused world Mr. Wilde depicts so cleverly, so mercilessly. The special fascination of the piece is, of course, just there—at that point of contrast. Mr. Wilde's work may fairly claim to go with that of Edgar Poe, and with some good French work of the same kind, done, probably, in more or less conscious imitation of it.

—Walter Pater, "A Novel by Mr. Wilde,"
1891, *Sketches and Reviews*, 1919, pp. 126–133

INTENTIONS

Richard Le Gallienne (1891)

Richard Le Gallienne was a poet and essayist, a probable lover of Wilde's, and a young man strongly influenced by Wilde's artistic style and views when he arrived on the London literary scene. He was a member of the Rhymer's Club, the early 1890s poetic circle highly influenced by aestheticism. He also contributed to the *Yellow Book*, a publication known for its promotion of the artistic philosophy of the 1890s.

In this extract, Le Gallienne treats two important aspects of Wilde's collection of essays, *Intentions*: its humor and Wilde's use of language. Of the former, Le Gallienne suggests that Wilde is always gently laughing at his readers, treating artistic criticism as an elaborate receptacle for displaying his singular wit. He sees in Wilde's use of language a "paradoxical method" playing off "the convertibility of terms." Critics have always addressed Wilde's use of language, his witticisms, puns, reversals of meaning, and his paradoxes, assessing them as proof of his genius, his art's shallowness, or, usually, a position somewhere between these two extremes. Le Gallienne appreciates that often Wilde's humor masks the underlying seriousness of his statements, and critics today often address the staking out of important ethical and aesthetic positions in many of Wilde's witticisms. The ability to play with the signification of language, the fact that words are not inescapably tied to definite meanings, is a very modern attitude to strike, one that students might employ to examine Wilde's relevance to contemporary theoretical approaches to language.

Mr. Wilde, in speaking of the methods open to the critic, well says that Mr. Pater's narrative is, of course, only criticism in disguise: his figures are but personifications of certain moods of mind, in which he is for the time interested, and which he desires express. Now I have been wondering whether one should not, similarly, regard Mr. Wilde essentially as a humorist who has taken art-criticism for his medium, just as Carlyle was a humorist in the odd disguise of a prophet. Certainly, I am inclined to think that much of his intricate tracery of thought and elaborate jewel-work of expression is simply built up to make a casket for one or two clever homeless paradoxes. "The fact of a man being a poisoner is nothing against his prose." Mr. Wilde somehow struck that out, and saw that it was deserving of a better fate than to remain a waif of traditionary epigram; so he went to work on Lamb's strange friend, Thomas Griffiths Wainewright, one of the subtlest art-critics and poisoners of his time, unearthed his curious history, made selections from his criticism, and then set his own epigram, diamond-wise, in the midst of a biographical essay. Various readers solemnly add to their historical knowledge, discuss the strange character of the man, study his criticism; but Mr. Wilde sits and watches his epigram sparkling far within. About Wainewright he cares far less than the reader, about his own epigram—far more.

Of course this is not the whole truth about these *Intentions;* the whole truth is a many-coloured thing about a personality so complex as that of the author of *Dorian Gray.* But it is the dominant tendency among many others hardly less powerful. Mr. Wilde's worship of beauty is proverbial, it has made a latter-day myth of him before his time; and yet, at least in these essays, his gift of comic perception is above it, and, rightly viewed, all his "flute-toned" periods are written in the service of the comic muse. Where he is not of malice aforethought humorous, where he seems to be arguing with serious face enough, is it not simply that he may smile behind his mask at the astonishment, not to say terror, of a public he has from the first so delighted in shocking? He loves to hear it call him "dangerous," as some men delight to be called "roue."

There will be many who will, as the phrase is, take him seriously; but let me assure them that Mr. Wilde is not of the number. It all depends what one means by the phrase; for I, for one, take Mr. Wilde very seriously as a creator of work which gives me much and various new pleasure: he is so absolutely alive at every point, so intensely practical—if people could only see it—and therefore so refreshingly unsentimental; he is wittier than is quite fair in a man of his nationality, and he often writes prose that one loves to say over for mere pleasure of ear—his own literary touchstone. The artistic temperament should delight in him, for the serious in the pursuit of literary pleasure he is as serious as every new joy must be; it is only in the domain of thought where it is rather funny to see him taken with such open mouth. Not that Mr. Wilde

is not a thinker, and a very subtle one too; but it is rather, so to say, as a
damascener of thought, than a forger of it, that he is to be regarded. . . .

It belongs to Mr. Wilde's paradoxical method that he should continually
play on the convertibility of terms. Thus, the whole contention of his essays
on criticism is that criticism and creation are essentially one and the same, or,
at least, that they necessarily dovetail one into the other; and yet towards the
end of this essay we find Gilbert saying "it is certain that the subject-matter
at the disposal of creation is always diminishing, while the subject-matter of
criticism increases daily." Here we have the two terms crystallised once more
to their hard and fast everyday meaning, while all through they have been
used as convertible. This is apt to bewilder. As a rule, however, Mr. Wilde
gains his effects by adhering to the concrete signification of words. This
reduces some of his contentions to a mere question of terms. One often feels:
Now, if that word were but changed for another, for which it really stands,
there would be nothing further to say. But that, of course, would not do
for Mr. Wilde, nor, indeed, for us, to whom, presumably, subject is nought
and treatment is all. Occasionally, by this means, it follows that Mr. Wilde
seems to beg the question; as, for instance, in his remarks on morality in
art. When he says, "All art is immoral," he is using the word in its narrow
relative sense; he does not mean by it the same as those who use it seriously
against certain schools and forms of art: though they say "immoral" they
mean "unspiritual," and that is the meaning many people will attach to the
word in Mr. Wilde's phrase. They will thus be quite unnecessarily shocked
by a mere quibble of words, and their real position is left unassailed; the real
question at issue being whether or not there is certain art which is dangerous
to the spirit, of which one should feel as Mr. Pater says in *Marius:* "This is
what I may not look at." If life be really a struggle between higher and lower,
if art is anything more than a form of sensuous indulgence, this is a question
to be answered. Mr. Wilde does not leave us quite clear as to his side in the
matter, though he seems to lay over-much stress on the sensuous side of art,
a side which is, after all, external and impossible without an informing,
formative soul. He echoes, too, Gautier's tirades against "virtue," and Mr.
Swinburne's

> What ailed us, oh gods, to desert you
> For the creeds that refuse and restrain?

and says hard things of chastity and self-sacrifice—really a very "young" and
quite illogical position in an age which has accepted evolution. He quotes
M. Renan to the effect that "Nature cares little about chastity"; but does

that prove anything save that Nature is always behind the age, as Mr. Wilde tells us in another place? Surely it is by such ideals, of which, once seen, the beauty haunts him through all his sinnings, that man evolves at all, striving and failing and striving, till slowly what was once the ideal becomes the instinct.

But I am not recking my own rede, and am in danger of growing quite "heated," as they say of politicians, while Mr. Wilde is doubtless smiling in his sleeve.

Let us leave contention and enjoy. I have referred to two or three of the interesting qualities in these papers. They are so absolutely alive. Every sentence is full of brain. There is no padding, no vagueness, all is "thought out," as the painters say. One has that safe, untroubled feeling in reading that Matthew Arnold's calm dissecting method gives us—though, needless to say, the austerity of the *Essays in Criticism* is a very different thing from this luxuriously coloured prose: however difficult the thesis, we leave it to the writer with perfect confidence that he will speedily make all clear. Mr. Wilde has, indeed, a rare power of keeping his eye steadily "on the object." It is doubtless, too, a part of his perversity that while, as we have seen, he will, when it suits him, adhere rigidly to the fixed signification of words, he can at other times exercise a quite remarkable power of reducing them to their elements, of remorselessly forcing them to say what they really mean. "You must not be frightened by words," said Gilbert to his young neophyte; and certainly, if you set such words as "unpractical," "dangerous," or "dreamer" on to Mr. Wilde they will come in for the same summary dissection that befel the lion which attacked the strong man in Holy Writ.

—Richard Le Gallienne, *Academy,*
July 4, 1891, pp. 7–8

AGNES REPPLIER
"THE BEST BOOK OF THE YEAR" (1892)

Agnes Repplier was an American essayist, scholar, and humorist. In this extract, she praises the way Wilde's style set him apart from the mundane, realistic writing of their contemporaries and points out that rather than embodying the "spirit of his time," Wilde makes a philosophy of art's re-creation of the "facts" of history, the representation of the world as a beautiful object outside its "grayness" in actuality. Appreciating the telling of "beautiful, untrue things" in art is, for Repplier, Wilde's most important contribution to their age. His aesthetic "lies" allow one to survive what is otherwise the unendurable, tedious "truth" of life.

Ever since the first printers with misguided zeal dipped an innocent world in ink, those books have been truly popular which reflected faithfully and enthusiastically the foibles and delusions of the hour. This is what is called "keeping abreast with the spirit of the times," and we have only to look around us at present to see the principle at work. With an arid and dreary realism chilling us to the heart, and sad-voiced novelists entreating us at every turn to try to cultivate religious doubts, fiction has ceased to be a medium of delight. Even nihilism, which is the only form of relief that true earnestness permits, is capable of being overstrained, and some narrowly conservative people are beginning to ask themselves already whether this new development of "murder as a fine art" has not been sufficiently encouraged. Out of the midst of the gloom, out of the confusion and depression of conflicting forms of seriousness, rises from London a voice, clear, languid, musical, shaken with laughter, and speaking in strange sweet tones of art and beauty, and of that finer criticism which is one with art and beauty, and claims them forever as its own. The voice comes from Mr. Oscar Wilde, and few there are who listen to him, partly because his philosophy is alien to our prevalent modes of thought, and partly because of the perverse and paradoxical fashion in which he delights to give it utterance. People are more impressed by the way a thing is said than by the thing itself. A grave arrogance of demeanor, a solemn and self-assertive method of reiterating an opinion until it grows weighty with words, are weapons more convincing than any subtlety of argument. "As I have before expressed to the still reverberating discontent of two continents," this is the mode in which the public loves to have a statement offered to its ears, that it may gape, and wonder, and acquiesce.

Now, nothing can be further from such admirable solidity than Mr. Wilde's flashing sword-play, than the glee with which he makes out a case against himself, and then proceeds valiantly into battle. There are but four essays in his recent volume, rather vaguely called *Intentions*, and of these four only two have real and permanent value. "The Truth of Masks" is a somewhat trivial paper, inserted apparently to help fill up the book, and "Pen, Pencil, and Poison" is visibly lacking in sincerity. The author plays with his subject very much as his subject, "kind, light-hearted Wainewright," played with crime, and in both cases there is a subtle and discordant element of vulgarity. It is not given to our eminently

respectable age to reproduce that sumptuous and horror-laden atmosphere
which lends an artistic glamor to the poisonous court of the Medicis. This
"study in green" contains, however, some brilliant passages, and at least
one sentence—"The domestic virtues are not the true basis of art, though
they may serve as an excellent advertisement for second-rate artists"—
that must make Mr. George Moore pale with envy when he reflects that he
missed saying it, where it belongs, in his clever, truthful, ill-natured paper
on "Mummer-Worship."

The significance and the charm of Mr. Wilde's book are centred in its
opening chapter, "The Decay of Lying," reprinted from *The Nineteenth
Century,* and in the long two-part essay entitled "The Critic as Artist,"
which embodies some of his most thoughtful, serious, and scholarly work.
My own ineffable content rests with "The Decay of Lying," because under its
transparent mask of cynicism, its wit, its satire, its languid mocking humor,
lies clearly outlined a great truth that is slipping fast away from us,—the
absolute independence of art—art nourished by imagination and revealing
beauty. This is the hand that gilds the grayness of the world; this is the
voice that sings in flute tones through the silence of the ages. To degrade
this shining vision into a handmaid of nature, to maintain that she should
give us photographic pictures of an unlovely life, is a heresy that arouses
in Mr. Wilde an amused scorn which takes the place of anger. "Art," he
says, "never expresses anything but itself. It has an independent life, just
as Thought has, and develops purely on its own lines. It is not necessarily
realistic in an age of realism, nor spiritual in an age of faith. So far from
being the creation of its time, it is usually in direct opposition to it, and
the only history that it preserves for us is the history of its own progress."
That we should understand this, it is necessary to understand also the
"beautiful untrue things" which exist only in the world of fancy; the things
that are lies, and yet that help us to endure the truth. Mr. Wilde repudiates
distinctly and almost energetically all lying with an object, all sordid trifling
with a graceful gift. The lies of newspapers yield him no pleasure; the
lies of politicians are ostentatiously unconvincing; the lies of lawyers are
"briefed by the prosaic." He reviews the world of fiction with a swift and
caustic touch; he lingers among the poets; he muses rapturously over those
choice historic masterpieces, from Herodotus to Carlyle, where "facts are
either kept in their proper subordinate position, or else entirely excluded
on the general ground of dulness." He laments with charming frankness
the serious virtues of his age. "Many a young man," he says, "starts in life
with a natural gift for exaggeration which, if nurtured in congenial and

sympathetic surroundings, or by the imitation of the best models, might grow into something really great and wonderful. But, as a rule, he comes to nothing. He either falls into careless habits of accuracy, or takes to frequenting the society of the aged and the well-informed. Both things are equally fatal to his imagination, and in a short time he develops a morbid and unhealthy faculty of truth-telling, begins to verify all statements made in his presence, has no hesitation in contradicting people who are much younger than himself, and often ends by writing novels that are so like life that no one can possibly believe in their probability." Surely this paragraph has but one peer in the world of letters, and that is the immortal sentence wherein De Quincey traces the murderer's gradual downfall to incivility and procrastination.

"The Critic as Artist" affords Mr. Wilde less scope for his humor and more for his erudition, which, perhaps, is somewhat lavishly displayed. Here he pleads for the creative powers of criticism, for its fine restraints, its imposed self-culture, and he couches his plea in words as rich as music. Now and then, it is true, he seems driven by the whips of our modern Furies to the verge of things which are not his to handle—problems, social and spiritual, to which he holds no key. When this occurs, we can only wait with drooping heads and what patience we can muster until he is pleased to return to his theme; or until he remembers, laughing, how fatal is the habit of imparting opinions, and what a terrible ordeal it is to sit at table with the man who has spent his life in educating others rather than himself. "For the development of the race depends on the development of the individual, and where self-culture has ceased to be the ideal, the intellectual standard is instantly lowered, and often ultimately lost." I like to fancy the ghost of the late rector of Lincoln, of him who said that an appreciation of Milton was the reward of consummate scholarship, listening in the Elysian Fields, and nodding his assent to this much-neglected view of a much-disputed question. Everybody is now so busy teaching that nobody has any time to learn. We are growing rich in lectures, but poor in scholars, and the triumph of mediocrity is at hand. Mr. Wilde can hardly hope to become popular by proposing real study to people burning to impart their ignorance; but the criticism that develops in the mind a more subtle quality of apprehension and discernment is the criticism that creates the intellectual atmosphere of the age.

—Agnes Repplier, "The Best Book
of the Year," *North American Review*,
January 1892, pp. 97–100

A HOUSE OF POMEGRANATES

H.L. Menken "A House of Pomegranates" (1918)

Henry Louis Mencken was an American journalist, author, and editor. Menken considers *A House of Pomegranates* as Wilde's foremost statement of an aesthetic philosophy, the best example of Wilde's art in that the text does not preach but rather embodies an attitude allowing the world to be perceived as an aesthetic spectacle. This attitude Menken believed to be Wilde's denial of what is called in the extract below a moral order, an order that Menken sees as the most fundamental belief of Anglo-Saxon peoples. The extract suggests that Wilde was not destroyed in court because of his sexual conduct, rather that his conduct was *used* to destroy him for his real crime: challenging the basic precepts of a society and seeking to create a new way of looking at the world, not as a moral system, but in terms of its beauty.

Wilde is here described as an anti-Puritan, but Menken interestingly suggests that the inherent flaw in Wilde's character and his art actually proceeded from his northern Scots-Irish Protestant heritage and its fundamentally puritanical character. In essence, Menken claims that Wilde was torn in his character and his art between attacking the puritanical order and doing so from a puritanical position. Wilde was revolted by the moral order he sought to subvert. It is because Menken sees in *A House of Pomegranates* the least evidence of this moral revulsion that he praises it for maintaining a more fundamentally aesthetic character than all the rest of Wilde's work. Menken describes the text as affording the reader the greatest example of color and warmth and form that he has recognized in modern English.

A House of Pomegranates was done almost exactly at the middle point of Wilde's career as an author, and in the days, coincidently, of his soundest and least perturbed celebrity. His poems, his posturings and his high services to W. S. Gilbert and to *Punch* were beginning to recede; ahead of him were *Salomé*, the four West End comedies, and catastrophe. Relatively placid waters surrounded him, shining in the sun. He had been married, and had got over it. There was a pleasant jingle of gold, or, at all events, of silver in his pocket. The foremost reviews of the day were open to him. He was not only a popular success, a figure in the public eye; he was, more importantly, beginning to get the attention of men of sense, to be taken with growing seriousness, to feel firm ground under him. And in age he was thirty-six, with the gas of youth oozed out and the stiffening of the climacteric not yet set in.

So situated, pleasantly becalmed between two storms, he wrote *A House of Pomegranates*, and into it, I have always believed, he put the most accurate and, on the whole, the most ingratiating revelation of his essential ideas that was ever to get upon paper. And without, of course, stating them at all—not a hint of exposition, of persuasion, of pedagogy is in the book. But that is precisely what gives them, there, their clarity and validity; they are not spoken for, they speak for themselves—and this is always the way a man sets forth the faith that is in him most honestly and most illuminatingly, not by arguing for it like some tin-pot evangelist, but by exhibiting it like an artist. Here we have the authentic Wilde, the Wilde who explains and dignifies all the lesser and more self-conscious Wildes. He is simply one who stands ecstatic before a vision of prodigious and almost intolerable beauty, a man haunted by ineffable magnificences of color, light, mass and line, a rapt and garrulous drunkard of the eye. He is one who apprehended loveliness in the world, not as sound, not as idea, not as order, not as syllogism, above all, not as law, but as picture pure and simple—as an ocular image leaping with life, gorgeous in its variety, infinite in its significances. And in the face of that enchanting picture, standing spellbound before its eloquent and narcotic forms, responding with all senses to its charming and intricate details, he appears before us as the type of all that the men of his race and time were not—as a rebel almost colossal in the profound artlessness of his denial. What he denied was the whole moral order of the world—the fundamental assumption of the Anglo-Saxon peoples. What he set up was a theory of the world as purely aesthetic spectacle, superb in its beauty, sufficiently its own cause and motive, ordered only by its own inner laws, and as innocent of all ethical import and utility as the precession of the equinoxes.

In this denial, of course, there was a challenge, and in that challenge was Wilde's undoing. To see him merely as a commonplace and ignoble misdemeanant, taken accidentally in some secret swinishness and condemned to a routine doom for that swinishness alone, is to accept a view of him that is impossibly journalistic and idiotic. He stood in the dock charged with a good deal more than private viciousness, and the punishment he got was a good deal more than private viciousness ever provokes, even from agents of the law who seek acquittal of themselves in their flogging of the criminal. What he was intrinsically accused of, and what he was so barbarously punished for, was a flouting of the premises upon which the whole civilization of his time was standing—a blasphemous attempt upon the gods that all docile and well-disposed men believed in, even in the midst of disservice—an heretical preaching of predicates and valuations that threatened to make a new generation see the world in a new way, to the unendurable confusion of the old one. In brief, his true trial was in the character of a heretic, and the case before the actual jury was no more than a symbol of a quite medieval summoning of the secular arm. What the secular arm thought of it I have often wondered—so astoundingly vast a hub-bub over an affair of everyday! Surely fish of precisely the same spots were coming into the net constantly, and in the sea of London there were many more, and some much larger to the eye. But Wilde, in truth, was the largest of them all. He had been marked for a long while, and delicately pursued. Lines had been cast for him; watchers had waited; there was a sort of affrighted and unspoken vow to dispose of him. And so, when he was hauled in at last, it was a good deal more than the mere taking of another spotted fish.

Thus I see the whole transaction, so obscenely wallowed in by the indignant and unintelligent, and thus I see Wilde himself—as one who cried up too impudently, too eloquently, and, above all, too persuasively a philosophy that was out of its time. As formidably ardent and potent upon the other side, I haven't the slightest doubt that his pathological sportings in the mire might have gone unchallenged, or at all events unwhooped. One hears of such things in Y. M. C. A. 's often enough, but in whispers; the very newspapers show discretion; surely no great state trials ensue. But here was a man who had done a great deal more than bring a passing stench into the synagogue. Here was one who had brought a scarlet woman there, and paraded her up and down, and shoved the croaking *Iokanaan* back into his rain-barrel, and invited the young men to consider the dignity and preciousness of beauty, and fluttered even the old ones with his Byzantine tales. Here, in brief, was one to be put down in swift dudgeon if disaster was to be avoided—if the concept of life as a bondage to implacable law was to stand unshaken—if the moral order of the world, or, at least, of that little corner of it, was to hold out against a stealthy and abominable paganism. Wilde was the first unmistakable anti-Puritan, the first uncompromising enemy of the essential Puritan character—the fear of beauty. He was destroyed, on the one hand, because he was getting power. He was destroyed, on the other hand, because he was fundamentally weak.

That weakness resided, in part, in a childish vanity, an empty desire for superficial consideration, that was peculiar to the man, but the rest of it, and perhaps the larger part, had deeper roots. It belonged to his race, to the ineradicable Scotticism of the North of Ireland Protestant; one perceives the same quality, lavishly displayed, in George Bernard Shaw—a congenital Puritanism beneath the surface layer of anti-Puritanism, a sort of moral revolt against the moral axiom, a civil war with fortunes that vary curiously, and often astonishingly. Wilde, as a youth, went to Greece with Mahaffy, and came home a professed Greek, but underneath there were always Northern reservations, a Northern habit of conscience, a Northern incapacity for Mediterranean innocence. One gets here, it seems to me, an explanation of many things—his squeamishness in certain little ways (all his work, in phrase, is as 'clean' as Walter Pater's or Leonardo's); his defective grasp of the concept of honor, as opposed to that of morals; the strange limits set upon his aesthetic reactions (e.g., his anesthesia to music); his touches of grossness; his inability to distinguish between aristocracy and mere social consideration; most of all, that irrepressible inner reminder which led him constantly to stand aghast, so to speak, before his own heresies—that pressing and ineradicable sense of their diabolism. In a word, the man was quite unable to throw off his inheritance entirely. It dogged him in the midst of his prosperity. It corrupted his sincerity. It sent doubts to tease him, and flung him into hollow extravagances of self-assertion. And when, in the end, he faced a tremendous and inexorable issue, he met it in an almost typically Puritanical manner—that is, timorously, evasively, dishonestly, with an eye upon the crowd, almost morally—as you will find set forth at length, if you are interested, in Frank Harris' capital biography.

In a word, Wilde was, at bottom, a second-rate man, and so inferior to his cause that he came near ditching it. One gets, from the accounts of those who were in close relations with him, a feeling of repugnance like that bred by the familiar 'good man'; he was, on his plane, as insufferable as a Methodist is on his. But there was in him something that is surely not in the Methodist, and that was a capacity for giving his ideas a dignity not in himself—a talent as artist which, at its best, was almost enough to conceal his limitations as a man. What he did with words was a rare and lovely thing. Himself well-nigh tone-deaf, he got into them a sonorous and majestic music. Himself hideous, he fashioned them into complex and brilliant arabesques of beauty. Himself essentially shallow and even bogus, he gave them thunderous eloquence, an austere dignity almost Biblical, the appearance of high sincerity that goes with all satisfying art. In these stories, I believe, he is at his best. His mere flashiness is reduced to very little; his ideas, often hollow, are submerged in feelings; he seems to forget his followers, his place, his celebrity, and to devote himself wholly to his work; he is the artist emancipated, for the moment, from the other things

that he was, and the worse things that he tried to be. I know of no modern
English that projects color and warmth and form more brilliantly, or that
serves more nobly the high purposes of beauty, or that stands further from
the flaccid manner and uses of everyday stupidity. There are faults in it, true
enough. At times it grows self-conscious, labored, almost sing-song. But in
the main it is genuinely distinguished—in the main it is signal work.

> —H.L. Menken, "A House of Pomegranates,"
> Introduction, New York, 1918, pp. i–viii

SALOMÉ

LORD ALFRED DOUGLAS (1893)

Wilde's play *Salomé* was banned from the stage, as mentioned in this
extract written by Alfred Douglas for the Oxford aesthetic journal
Spirit Lamp. E.F.S. Pigott, the English licenser of plays, was able to ban
it because of an obscure law that refused to allow the presentation of
biblical characters onstage. Douglas scathingly addresses the rationale
behind this ban, along with offering an appreciation of the text of the
play itself. Largely because of his happiness with the article, and no
doubt to help his unpublished lover enter the London literary world,
Wilde asked Douglas to translate the play from the French, in which it
was initially written, into English. Unfortunately, Douglas's French was
inadequate to the task, and, in his usual fashion, the young lord refused
to recognize any incapacity on his own part. Wilde and Douglas would
have one of their several, recurring, and serious arguments over the
translation. Wilde's friend Robert Ross also became embroiled, and this
began Douglas's jealousy of and antipathy toward Ross.

The play was never written to be performed, and Douglas remarks
on his appreciation of seemingly *listening* to Wilde's French as the play
is read, the musical quality of the language, its tones and nuanced
deployment of manner and style. The play was hailed as a great work in
the less conservative literary world of Paris, which argues that the type
of praise heaped on Wilde in this extract is perhaps not as exaggerated
as it first seems. Concluding that to the English world of "roast beef
and Bible" the play is morbid and unhealthy, Douglas states it could be
nothing less, considering the story it represents; but it is simultaneously
a noble theme and one that only those who joyously engage in life can
appreciate. Douglas attacks the tawdry working-class farces and their

low, vulgar sensibilities; equally he attacks those "muscular Christians," specifically the novelist Charles Kingsley, who promoted a strident, manly form of Anglican Christianity as "healthy" in contrast to the "poisonous" aestheticism of the period.

⚜ ⚜ ⚜

That mouthpiece of Philistinism, the daily press, surpassed itself in the stern and indignant condemnation of the book which it had not read and the play which it had not seen; never before it declared had such an outrage on decency and good taste been committed, never had a more infamous plot against morality and the Bible been nipped in the bud. For it *was* nipped in the bud, the censor had refused to license its production, England was saved from lasting disgrace. The daily press positively swelled with pride, it metaphorically slapped its chest and thanked God it was an Englishman. It is hard to understand the attitude taken up by the anonymous scribblers who propounded these pompous absurdities. Why it should be taken for granted that because a writer takes his subject from a sublime and splendid literature, he should necessarily treat it in a contemptible manner, is a mystery it is hard to solve. Apparently it never occurred to these enlightened beings that the very sublimity and grandeur of such a subject would be a sufficient guarantee that the artist had put his very best work into it, and had done his utmost to exalt his treatment to the high level his subject demanded. To a man who takes for the scene of a vulgar farce, the back drawing-room of a house in Bloomsbury, and who brings on to the stage a swindling stockbroker or a rag-and-bone merchant, they are ready to listen with delighted attention, to laugh at his coarse jokes and revel in his cockney dialogue; good healthy English fun they call it. But a man who actually takes for the scene of a tragedy the gorgeous background of a Roman Tetrarch's court, and who brings on to the stage a real prophet out of the Bible, and all in French too! 'No, it is too much,' they say, 'we don't want to hear anything more about it, it is an outrage and an infamy.' O Happy England, land of healthy sentiment, roast beef and Bible, long may you have such men to keep guard over your morals, to point out to you the true path, and to guide your feet into the way of cant! (…)

One thing strikes one very forcibly in the treatment, the musical form of it. Again and again it seems to one that in reading one is *listening*; listening, not to the author, not to the direct unfolding of a plot, but to the tones of different instruments, suggesting, suggesting, always indirectly, till one feels that by shutting one's eyes one can best catch the suggestion. The author's personality nowhere shews itself.

The French is as much Mr. Wilde's own as is the psychological motive of the play, it is perfect in scholarship, but it takes a form new in French literature. It is a daring experiment and a complete success. The language is rich and coloured, but never precious, and shows a command of expression so full and varied that the ascetically artistic restraint of certain passages stands out in strong relief. Such a passage is the one quoted above: the conversation of the soldiers on the terrace; in which by-the-by certain intelligent critics have discovered a resemblance to Ollendorf, and with extraordinary shallowness and lack of artistic sensibility have waxed facetious over. O wonderful men!

Artistically speaking the play would gain nothing by performance, to my mind it would lose much. To be appreciated it must be abstracted, and to be abstracted it must be read. Let it, 'not to the sensual ear but more endeared, pipe to the spirit ditties of no tone.'

It only remains to say that the treatment of St. John the Baptist is perfectly refined and reverend.

I suppose the play is unhealthy, morbid, unwholesome, and un-English, ça va sans dire. It is certainly un-English, because it is written in French, and therefore unwholesome to the average Englishman, who can't digest French. It is probably morbid and unhealthy, for there is no representation of quiet domestic life, nobody slaps anybody else on the back all through the play, and there is not a single reference to roast beef from one end of the dialogue to the other, and though it is true that there is a reference to Christianity, there are no muscular Christians. Anyone, therefore, who suffers from that most apalling and widespread of diseases which takes the form of a morbid desire for health had better avoid and flee from *Salomé*, or they will surely get a shock that it will take months of the daily papers and Charles Kingsley's novels to counteract. But the less violently and aggressively healthy, those who are healthy to live and do not live to be healthy, will find in Mr. Oscar Wilde's tragedy the beauty of a perfect work of art, a joy for ever, ambrosia to feed their souls with honey of sweet-bitter thoughts.

—Lord Alfred Douglas,
Spirit Lamp, May 1893, pp. 21–27

EDWARD E. HALE, JR.
"SIGNS OF LIFE IN LITERATURE" (1894)

In this extract, the American critic Edward Hale, Jr. suggests that Wilde's *Salomé* will not last in the literary world. He claims it is "ephemeral" but recognizes in its dialogue, despite its affectations, a spirit of life that he finds "curiously moved." It is Hale's comments on the English artist Aubrey Beardsley and his critique of Beardsley and Wilde as the same artistic type that are his most insightful observations. The "protean" (changing and changeable) nature of the two, their capacity to avoid definition because of their constant adoption of various styles, masks, and manners seen in art, lead Hale to suggest that someone should determine and fix, if only for an instant, the aesthetic quality that both share. Students might consider, in light of Hale's suggestion and those of several earlier extracts, whether this changeability might itself be the fundamental quality behind the personalities of Wilde the man, as much as being the underlying reason for the vastly varying interpretations of Wilde's art.

Mr. Oscar Wilde never troubles one with taking himself too seriously, and the history of *Salomé* is Oscar Wilde all over. It was written in French and produced in Paris. Desirous then of favoring his own countrymen, Mr. Wilde made preparation to present it in London. In this worthy attempt, however, he was hindered—so the papers told us—by some official folly which enraged him so much that he was even strongly tempted to stop being an Englishman, in favor of that less imbecile people across the Channel. But not wishing to keep his anger forever, Mr. Wilde finally allowed his noble friend Lord Alfred Bruce Douglas to do the play into English. It was then "pictured," as the phrase is, by Mr. Aubrey Beardsley, and is now ready for the delight of a somewhat indifferent world.

Such an extraordinary conjunction of affections is ominous. But, strangely enough, there are some things in *Salomé* that are good. It is impossible to read it without feeling curiously moved and stirred. The careless talk of the loungers on the terrace, the soldiers and the Cappadocian, is good; the squabbling of the Jews, the Pharisee, the Sadducee, the Nazarene, is good. So, also, is Herod,— indeed the character of Herod is quite the best conceived thing in the play, as his description of his treasure is the best written. The play may well have been very effective on the stage, for there is a constant feeling of movement, of life, and it is certainly worth reading now that it is published.

With all this, however, the play is wholly ephemeral. Its action is trivial and its dialogue affected. Its ideas, and its language too, are extravagances, without much more foundation than the extravagances of Mr. Hamlin Garland. But while in Mr. Garland we have the prophet of Literature as Life, we have in Mr. Wilde the follower of Literature as Art. Mr. Garland is a "veritist," and prefers the fresh novelties of nature. But Mr. Wilde seeks beauty, in art and art's most latent subtleties. He contrives expressions and conceptions of the most curious and self-conscious refinement, of the strangest and most ultra-precious distinction. As ever, he scorns the ordinary, the every-day, the generally pleasing, and is unremitting to attain the romantic beauty, the strange, the wonderful, the remote, the reward of no art but the most devoted, the delight of no taste but the most distinguished.

As such, his work lends itself eminently to the illustration of Mr. Aubrey Beardsley. Mr. Aubrey Beardsley receives a good many hard words nowadays,— and certainly his pictures are strange things, more affected than Oscar Wilde himself, and more remote from obvious apprehension. What one is first inclined to criticise in Mr. Beardsley is his lack of originality. His pictures remind us of almost every phase of art that has ever existed; or, at any rate, of every phase which had ever a tinge of the grotesque or the trivial in its character. From the bald priestly pictures mingled among Egyptian hieroglyphics, down to the graceful frivolities of Willette of the Red Windmill, Mr. Beardsley seems to have laid everything under contribution. His work seems by turns one thing and then another—Japanese, Gothic, Preraphaelite, what you will. So it seems at first. But the great excellence is that, however Protean, Mr. Aubrey Beardsley, like Satan in *Paradise Lost*, is always himself, even in the midst of his disguises. Just what is his own quality, is hard to say; but there can be little doubt that it exists, and it would be worth somebody's while to determine it in the shifting dazzle of his influences,—to fix it for an instant for us, to get its true character and flavor unadulterated. But whatever be his quality, it is eminently in keeping with the work of Mr. Oscar Wilde.

—Edward E. Hale Jr., "Signs of Life in
Literature," *Dial*, July 1, 1894, pp. 12–13

A WOMAN OF NO IMPORTANCE
AND AN IDEAL HUSBAND

WILLIAM ARCHER
"A WOMAN OF NO IMPORTANCE" (1893)

William Archer was a Scottish drama critic, author, and the translator of Henrik Ibsen's plays. Despite his promotion of the modernist Ibsen, Archer displayed admiration for Wilde as a playwright; he had been, with Bernard Shaw, critical of the English licenser of plays for refusing to permit a staging of *Salomé*.

In this extract, Archer praises Wilde's theater writing as standing alone at the highest level of English drama. While he does not think that Wilde's *A Woman of No Importance* is a masterpiece, he believes it to be proportionately better than any other English work of the period. It is not for his wit that Archer singles Wilde out for the highest praise but for his thoughtful and original perspective on life, his verbal style, and primarily for his appreciation of the "dramatic instinct" itself. The extract offers students an example of a detailed analysis of one of Wilde's plays, written by one of his most widely read contemporary theater critics.

———————

There is no such thing as "absolute pitch" in criticism; the intervals are everything. In other words, the critic is bound to deal in odious comparisons; it is one of the painful necessities of his calling. He must clearly indicate the plane, so to speak, on which, in his judgment, any given work of art is to be taken; and the value of his terms, whether of praise or blame, must then be estimated in relation to that plane. Well, the one essential fact about Mr Oscar Wilde's dramatic work is that it must be taken on the very highest plane of modern English drama, and furthermore, that it stands alone on that plane. In intellectual calibre, artistic competence—ay, and in dramatic instinct to boot—Mr Wilde has no rival among his fellow-workers for the stage. He is a thinker and a writer; they are more or less able, thoughtful, original playwrights. This statement may seem needlessly emphatic, and even offensive; but it is necessary that it should be made if we are to preserve any sense of proportion in criticism. I am far from exalting either *Lady Windermere's Fan* or *A Woman of No Importance* to the rank of a masterpiece; but while we carp at this point and cavil at that, it behoves us to remember and to avow that we are dealing with works of an altogether higher order than others which we may very likely have praised with much less reserve.

Pray do not suppose that I am merely dazzled by Mr Wilde's pyrotechnic wit. That is one of the defects of his qualities, and a defect, I am sure, that he will one day conquer, when he begins to take himself seriously as a dramatic artist. At present, he approaches his calling as cynically as Mr George R. Sims; only it is for the higher intellects, and not the lower, among the play-going public, that Mr Wilde shows his polite contempt. He regards prose drama (so he has somewhere stated) as the lowest of the arts; and acting on this principle—the falsity of which he will discover as soon as a truly inspiring subject occurs to him—he amuses himself by lying on his back and blowing soap-bubbles for half an evening, and then pretending, during the other half, to interest himself in some story of the simple affections such as audiences, he knows, regard as dramatic. Most of the soap bubbles are exceedingly pretty, and he throws them off with astonishing ease and rapidity—

One *mot* doth tread upon another's heels, So fast they follow—

but it becomes fatiguing, in the long run, to have the whole air a-shimmer, as it were, with iridescent films. Mr Wilde will one day be more sparing in the quantity and more fastidious as to the quality of his wit, and will cease to act up to Lord Illingworth's motto that "nothing succeeds like excess." It is not his wit, then, and still less his knack of paradox-twisting, that makes me claim for him a place apart among living English dramatists. It is the keenness of his intellect, the individuality of his point of view, the excellence of his verbal style, and, above all, the genuinely dramatic quality of his inspirations. I do not hesitate to call the scene between Lord Illingworth and Mrs Arbuthnot at the end of the second act of this play the most virile and intelligent—yes, I mean it, the most intelligent—piece of English dramatic writing of our day. It is the work of a man who knows life, and knows how to transfer it to the stage. There is no situation-hunting, no posturing. The interest of the scene arises from emotion based upon thought, thought thrilled with emotion. There is nothing conventional in it, nothing insincere. In a word, it is a piece of adult art. True, it is by far the best scene in the play, the only one in which Mr Wilde does perfect justice to his talent. But there are many details of similar, though perhaps not equal, value scattered throughout. How fine and simple in its invention, for instance, is the scene in which the mother tells her son the story of Lord Illingworth's treachery, only to hear him defend the libertine on the ground that no "nice girl" would have let herself be entrapped! This exquisite touch of ironic pathos is worth half a hundred "thrilling tableaux," like that which follows almost immediately upon it.

For it is not to be denied that in his effort to be human—I would say "to be popular," did I not fear some subtle and terrible vengeance on the part of the outraged author—Mr Wilde has become more than a little conventional. How different is the "He is your father!" tableau at the end of Act III from the strong and simple conclusion of Act II—how different, and how inferior! It would be a just retribution if Mr Wilde were presently to be confronted with this tableau, in all the horrors of chromolithography, on every hoarding in London, with the legend, "Stay, Gerald! He is your father!" in crinkly letters in the corner. Then, indeed, would expatriation—or worse—be the only resource of his conscience-stricken soul. His choice would lie between Paris and prussic acid.

The conventional element seems to me to come in with the character of Mrs Arbuthnot. Why does Mr Wilde make her such a terribly emphatic personage? Do ladies in her (certainly undesirable) position brood so incessantly upon their misfortune? I have no positive evidence to go upon, but I see no reason why Mrs Arbuthnot should not take a more common-sense view of the situation. That she should resent Lord Illingworth's conduct I quite understand, and I applaud the natural and dignified revenge she takes in declining to marry him. But why all this agony? Why all this hatred? Why can "no anodyne give her sleep, no poppies forgetfulness"? With all respect for Mrs Arbuthnot, this is mere empty phrase-making. I am sure she has slept very well, say, six nights out of the seven, during these twenty years; or, if not, she has suffered from a stubborn determination to be unhappy, for which Lord Illingworth can scarcely be blamed. After all, what material has she out of which to spin twenty years of unceasing misery? She is—somehow or other—in easy circumstances; she has a model son to satisfy both her affections and her vanity; it does not even appear that she is subjected to any social slights or annoyances. A good many women have led fairly contented lives under far more trying conditions. Perhaps Mr Wilde would have us believe that she suffers from mild religious mania—that it is the gnawing thought of her unpardonable "sin" that nor poppy nor mandragora can soothe. But she herself admits that she does not repent the "sin" that has given her a son to love. Well then, what is all this melodrama about? Does not Mrs Arbuthnot sacrifice our interest, if not our sympathy, by her determination "in obstinate condolement to persever"? May we not pardonably weary a little (to adapt Lord Illingworth's saying) of "the Unreasonable eternally lamenting the Unalterable"? Mrs Arbuthnot is simply a woman who has been through a very painful experience, who has suffered a crushing disappointment in the revelation of the unworthiness of the man she loved, but for whom life, after all, has turned out not so very intolerably. That is the rational view of her situation; and she herself might quite well take that view without the sacrifice of one scene or speech of any real value. The masterly scene at the end of the second act would remain practically intact, and so would the scene between mother and son in the third act; for the complacent cruelty of Gerald's commentary on her story could not but cause a bitter pang to any mother. It is only in the fourth act that any really important alteration would be necessary, and there it could only be for the better. The young man's crude sense of the need for some immediate and heroic action is admirably conceived, and entirely right; but how much better, how much truer, how much newer, would the scene be if the mother met his Quixotism with sad, half-smiling dignity and wisdom, instead of with passionate outcries of unreasoning horror! There

is a total lack of irony, or, in other words, of commonsense, in this portion of
the play. Heroics respond to heroics, until we feel inclined to beg both mother
and son (and daughter-in-law, too, for that matter) to come down from their
stilts and look at things a little rationally. Even Mr Wilde's writing suffers. We
are treated to such noble phrases as "I am not worthy or of her or of you,"
and it would surprise no one if Master Gerald were to drop into blank verse
in a friendly way. How much more telling, too, would the scene between
Mrs Arbuthnot and Lord Illingworth become if she took the situation more
ironically and less tragically, if she answered the man of the world in the tone
of a woman of the world! How much more complete, for one thing, would be
his humiliation! As it is, the vehemence of her hatred can only minister to his
vanity. From the point of view of vanity, to be hated for twenty years is just
as good as to be loved. It is indifference that stings. It was all very well, in the
second act, for Mrs Arbuthnot to be vehement in her protest against the father's
annexation of the son; in the fourth act, when that danger is past, a tone of calm
superiority would be ten times as effective. In short, the play would have been
a much more accomplished work of art if the character of Mrs Arbuthnot had
been pitched in another key. And I am not without a suspicion that Mr Wilde's
original design was something like what I have indicated. The last word spoken,
"A man of no importance" (which was doubtless the first word conceived)
seems to belong to the woman I imagine rather than to the one who actually
speaks it. I think, too, that the concluding situation would be more effective if
some more definite indication of the unspeakable cad who lurks beneath Lord
Illingworth's polished surface were vouchsafed us earlier in the play. True, his
conduct towards the fair American was sufficiently objectionable; but I fear I,
for my part, did not quite seriously believe in it, taking it rather as a mere *ficelle*,
and not a very ingenious one, leading up to the startling picture-poster at the
end of the third act.

—William Archer, "*A Woman of
No Importance,*" 1893, *The Theatrical
"World" of 1893,* 1894, pp. 105–112

George Bernard Shaw "Two New Plays" (1895)

George Bernard Shaw was a leading drama critic in the 1890s and
became one of the best-known twentieth-century dramatists in his own
right. He was Irish and an active socialist, and he found in drama a form
through which he could present his political views to Victorian audiences
not generally known for their radical sympathies. Here he examines

Wilde's plays and, at the same time, mocks the incapacity of the English to appreciate Wilde's playfulness. Students might consider Shaw's more general attack on the English character, considering that this review was written shortly before Wilde's trials. Comparisons with earlier extracts written by fellow Irishmen Joyce and Yeats at different periods offer interesting points of comparison and contrast.

Wilde had said, "All art is completely useless," and it therefore comes as something of a surprise to read a dramatist and political activist such as Shaw remarking that he views Wilde as, in some ways, England's only "thorough playwright." But Shaw means something quite particular: that Wilde is, first and foremost, playful in his dramas. It is precisely this quality that Shaw sees the English as failing to appreciate; he states that it infuriates middle-class English audiences and critics. On one hand, the English claim to want no didacticism (moral education) in their art, then fume and rage at Wilde for writing humorous plays. Shaw claims that to the English no nation is as foreign in temperament as that of the Irish (a fairly radical political statement as the two "nations" were then still united under the British crown). The self-important seriousness of the English is what Wilde teases in his plays and is equally the cause of the English becoming annoyed with him and his art.

Mr Oscar Wilde's new play at the Haymarket (*An Ideal Husband*) is a dangerous subject, because he has the property of making his critics dull. They laugh angrily at his epigrams, like a child who is coaxed into being amused in the very act of setting up a yell of rage and agony. They protest that the trick is obvious, and that such epigrams can be turned out by the score by any one lightminded enough to condescend to such frivolity. As far as I can ascertain, I am the only person in London who cannot sit down and write an Oscar Wilde play at will. The fact that his plays, though apparently lucrative, remain unique under these circumstances, says much for the self-denial of our scribes. In a certain sense Mr Wilde is to me our only thorough playwright. He plays with everything: with wit, with philosophy, with drama, with actors and audience, with the whole theatre. Such a feat scandalizes the Englishman, who can no more play with wit and philosophy than he can with a football or a cricket bat. He works at both, and has the consolation, if he cannot make people laugh, of being the best cricketer and footballer in the world. Now it is the mark of the artist that he will not work. Just as people with social ambitions will practise the meanest economies in order to live expensively; so the artist will starve his way through incredible toil and discouragement sooner than go and earn a week's honest wages. Mr Wilde, an arch-artist, is so colossally lazy that he trifles even with the work by which an artist escapes work. He distils the very quintessence, and gets as product plays which are so unapproachably playful that they are the delight of every playgoer with twopenn'orth of brains. The English critic, always protesting that the drama should not be didactic, and yet always complaining if the dramatist does not find sermons in stones and good in everything, will be conscious of a subtle and pervading levity in *An Ideal Husband*. All the literary dignity of the play, all the imperturbable good sense and good manners with which Mr Wilde makes his wit pleasant to his comparatively stupid audience, cannot quite overcome the fact that Ireland is of all countries the most foreign to England, and that to the Irishman (and Mr Wilde is almost as acutely Irish an Irishman as the Iron Duke of Wellington) there is nothing in the world quite so exquisitely comic as an Englishman's seriousness. It becomes tragic, perhaps, when the Englishman acts on it; but that occurs too seldom to be taken into account, a fact which intensifies the humor of the situation, the total result being the Englishman utterly unconscious of his real self, Mr Wilde keenly observant of it and playing on the self-unconsciousness with irresistible humor, and finally, of course, the Englishman annoyed with himself for being amused at his own expense, and for being unable to convict Mr Wilde of what seems an obvious misunderstanding of human nature. He is shocked, too, at the danger to the foundations of society when seriousness is publicly laughed at. And to complete the oddity of the situation, Mr Wilde, touching what he himself reverences, is absolutely the most sentimental dramatist of the day.

It is useless to describe a play which has no thesis: which is, in the purest integrity, a play and nothing less. The six worst epigrams are mere alms handed with a kind smile to the average suburban playgoer; the three best remain secrets between Mr Wilde and a few choice spirits. The modern note is struck in Sir Robert Chiltern's assertion of the individuality and courage of his wrongdoing as against the mechanical idealism of his stupidly good wife, and in his bitter criticism of a love that is only the reward of merit. It is from the philosophy on which this scene is based that the most pregnant epigrams in the play have been condensed. Indeed, this is the only philosophy that ever has produced epigrams. In contriving the stage expedients by which the action of the piece is kept going, Mr Wilde has been once or twice a little too careless of stage illusion: for example, why on earth should Mrs Cheveley, hiding in Lord Goring's room, knock down a chair? That is my sole criticism.

—George Bernard Shaw, "Two New Plays,"
1895, Works, 1930–38, vol. 23, pp. 9–11

THE IMPORTANCE OF BEING EARNEST

GEORGE BERNARD SHAW (1895)

George Bernard Shaw generally admired the art of Wilde's drama, but this review criticizes *The Importance of Being Earnest* as being akin to a farce from two decades earlier, as having a labored plot and dialogue, and exemplifying, despite what other critics had claimed as its ultramodernity, a type of old-fashioned drama devoid of contemporary value. While Bernard Shaw admits to being amused by the play, he remarks that, for an audience, finding amusement without being touched in any way makes a drama pointless. He finds himself laughing mechanically at the jokes, mirroring the staged mechanism of the story and humor. This response to *The Importance of Being Earnest* is an unusually critical one; most critics when it was first performed, as other extracts in this collection show, considered it Wilde's greatest artistic triumph. This stance, at least as far as Wilde's dramatic works are concerned, generally persists among critics today.

It is somewhat surprising to find Mr Oscar Wilde, who does not usually model himself on Mr Henry Arthur Jones, giving his latest play a five-chambered title like *The Case of Rebellious Susan*. So I suggest with some confidence that *The Importance of Being Earnest* dates from a period long anterior to *Susan*. However it may have been retouched immediately before its production, it must certainly have been written before *Lady Windermere's Fan*. I do not suppose it to be Mr Wilde's first play: he is too susceptible to fine art to have begun otherwise than with a strenuous imitation of a great dramatic poem, Greek or Shakespearian; but it was perhaps the first which he designed for practical commercial use at the West End theatres. The evidence of this is abundant. The play has a plot—a gross anachronism; there is a scene between the two girls in the second act quite in the literary style of Mr Gilbert, and almost inhuman enough to have been conceived by him; the humour is adulterated by stock mechanical fun to an extent that absolutely scandalizes one in a play with such an author's name to it; and the punning title and several of the more farcical passages recall the epoch of the late H. J. Byron. The whole has been varnished, and here and there veneered, by the author of *A Woman of No Importance*; but the general effect is that of a farcical comedy dating from the seventies, unplayed during that period because it was too clever and too decent, and brought up to date as far as possible by Mr Wilde in his now completely formed style. Such is the impression left by the play on me. But I find other critics, equally entitled to respect, declaring that *The Importance of Being Earnest* is a strained effort of Mr Wilde's at ultra-modernity, and that it could never have been written but for the opening up of entirely new paths in drama last year by *Arms and the Man*. At which I confess to a chuckle.

I cannot say that I greatly cared for *The Importance of Being Earnest*. It amused me, of course; but unless comedy touches me as well as amuses me, it leaves me with a sense of having wasted my evening. I go to the theatre to be moved to laughter, not to be tickled or bustled into it; and that is why, though I laugh as much as anybody at a farcical comedy, I am out of spirits before the end of the second act, and out of temper before the end of the third, my miserable mechanical laughter intensifying these symptoms at every outburst. If the public ever becomes intelligent enough to know when it is really enjoying itself and when it is not, there will be an end of farcical comedy. Now in *The Importance of Being Earnest* there is plenty of this rib-tickling: for instance, the lies, the deceptions, the cross purposes, the sham mourning, the christening of the two grown-up men, the muffin eating, and so forth. These could only have been raised from the farcical plane by making them occur to characters who had, like Don Quixote, convinced us of their reality and obtained some hold on our sympathy. But that unfortunate moment of Gilbertism breaks our belief in the humanity of the play. Thus we are thrown back on the force and daintiness of its wit, brought home by an exquisitely grave, natural, and unconscious execution on the part of the actors. . . . On the whole I must decline to accept *The Importance of Being Earnest* as a day less than ten years old; and I am altogether unable to perceive any uncommon excellence in its presentations.

—George Bernard Shaw, in *Saturday Review,*
February 23, 1895, lxxix, pp. 249–50,
reprinted in *Our Theatres in the Nineties,*
II, 1932, pp. 41–44

J.T. Grein "The Importance of Being Earnest" (1901)

J.T. Grein was the English critic for the *Sunday Times* and several other newspapers and the founder, in 1891, of the Independent Theatre which performed plays by Ibsen and Shaw turned down by mainstream, com-

mercial theaters. This extract was written on the reopening of Wilde's
The Importance of Being Earnest on the London stage in 1901. Even with
the play's reproduction, Wilde having died the year before, seven years
after his release from prison, Grein is annoyed to see that the theater has
avoided mentioning the dramatist's name on the program, instead mentioning another of Wilde's plays as a means of authorial identification
(even though *Earnest* was Wilde's finest drama).

Grein recalls the 1895 production and the praise it drew from audiences
at that time. He sees in *Earnest* an example of truly great dramatic comedy,
but a slight dropping off in quality with the third act (although he states
that this same act is better than another dozen comedies of the period).
The reason for this, Grein claims, is that the pressures of the events that
would lead to Wilde's downfall must have already been weighing heavily
on his mind. When so much philosophical criticism has been written
about the relationship between Wilde's life and his art, students might
consider the simple, often harsh, reality of personal stress on the life and
work of an artist.

A dead man's voice has been heard again, and as we listened to it the artist
himself once more stood before us. Forgotten was the history of the man,
forgotten the past. The hands of the clock had moved for seven years, but
the situation remained unchanged. Oscar Wilde has come to life again, and
on the night of December 2, when literary and social London foregathered
at the reproduction of *The Importance of Being Earnest,* there was celebrated a
feast of absolution, and, to a certain extent, of rehabilitation. In the midst of
our intellectual joy there sounded but two discordant notes—the one of anger,
the other of sadness. It made some of us angry to read on the programme
"The Importance of Being Earnest, by the author of *Lady Windermere's Fan,"*
whereby was indicated that, though it was good to use the artist's work, his
name was not sufficiently honourable to be given out to the public. I know
full well that the publisher has erred in this direction, as well as the manager,
but there is no excuse for either. The note of sadness was that so great a
mind as Oscar Wilde's had prematurely come to a standstill; that matters
independent of art had bereft us of the most brilliant wit of the period, and
that subsequent events, instead of leading to regeneration, brought a broken
career to an untimely termination.

In 1895, when *The Importance of Being Earnest* saw the light at the St.
James's Theatre, it was voted a perfect farce, and, but for the catastrophe, it
would have been played for centuries of evenings. I recall this not merely

as a chronological fact, but more particularly in order to emphasise the
exceeding cleverness of the play, since the duality of its fibre escaped most
of the critics, and certainly the majority of the public. The practised eye
discovered at once that the first and second acts and the third act were
not of the same mould. They made the impression of wines of different
vintages served in the same glasses. Those two acts—perfect, not only
as farce, but as comedy, too, for they reflect the manners of the period,
and are richly underlaid with humorous current—were written in days
when the poet basked in the hot sun of popularity, when his every saying
darted like an arrow through the land, when the whole of the English
speaking world echoed sallies which, though they were not always Oscar
Wilde's, were as *ben trovato* as if they had been his. The third act was—I
know it authoritatively—composed under stress of circumstances, when
the web was tightening round the man, and menaces of exposure must
have rendered his gaiety forced, like that of a being condemned to the
stocks. Under pressure a lofty mind often does excellent work, and it is
undeniable that in the third act of *The Importance of Being Earnest* there is
more cleverness than in one round dozen English comedies *en bloc*. There
are epigrams in it for the paternity of which some people would give a few
years of their lives, and as a solution to a tangle well-nigh inextricable it is
by no means unhappy. Yet it is not of the same quality as those other two
acts, in which the real, the probable, and the impossible form a *menage a
trois* of rare felicity. And as we listen to the play, what strikes us most of all
is not so much the utterances of a mind which could not fail to be brilliant,
but the prospect that this comedy—for I prefer to call it a comedy—will
enjoy a kind of perennial youth somewhat akin to Congreve's work or that
of Sheridan. It is a bold thing to say, I know, but if there is exaggeration,
let it pass, for the sake of the argument that when the artist's working
powers were shut off he had not yet thoroughly felt his feet, but was only
just beginning to plough his furrow in a new field. *The Importance of Being
Earnest* ranks high, not only on account of its gaiety—a gaiety which in
many produces the smile of intimate understanding, and in the less *blase*
guffaws straight from a happy mood—but because it satirises vividly,
pointedly, yet not unkindly, the mannerisms and foibles of a society which
is constantly before the public eye. I need not dive into details, for the plot
is, or ought to be, known to every lover of the Theatre. And I do not quote
epigrams, for it is but a poor glory to feather one's own cap with another
man's cleverness. Anon, when the play is revived at the St. James Theatre,
when the book of an author whose name one need no longer express with

bated breath, is sold by the thousand, there will be ample opportunity to refresh one's memory, and spend a joyful hour with *The Importance of Being Earnest.*

—J.T. Grein, *"The Importance of Being Earnest,"* 1901, *Dramatic Criticism,* 1902, vol. 3, pp. 264–266

MAX BEERBOHM "A CLASSIC FARCE" (1909)

Max Beerbohm writes this extracted review of another production of *The Importance of Being Earnest* in 1909, remarking on a distinction between Wilde's wit and humor as he had done in an earlier article cited in this volume. He calls the play a "farce," a popular type of drama from the 1870s onward and generally considered to be a low slapstick-style form of theater. But Beerbohm states that Wilde was able, through his skill, to turn this form into a "dazzling prism." He examines Wilde's wit and humor, the marriage of form and manner that Wilde was able to accomplish, as the basis for this magic-attributed transformation. Beerbohm mentions Wilde's earlier dramas, seeing a similar wit in them, but in which the critic can recognize the "mechanism" of plot. In *Earnest,* Wilde was able to dissolve the form of the story into the manner in which it is performed. Wilde is no Victorien Sardou, a successful, contemporary French dramatist believed by Beerbohm to have written plays in which the mechanical production of certain plot types is quite obvious. It is to Wilde's artistic credit that he has produced a farce that rises above the limits of its own form.

The Importance of Being Earnest has been revived by Mr Alexander at the St James's Theatre, and is as fresh and as irresistible as ever. It is vain to speculate what kind of work Oscar Wilde would have done had the impulse for play-writing survived in him. It is certain that a man of such variegated genius, and a man so inquisitive of art-forms, would not, as some critics seem to think he would, have continued to turn out plays in the manner of *The Importance of Being Earnest.* This, his last play, is not the goal at which he would have rested. But, of the plays that he wrote specifically for production in London theatres, it is the finest, the most inalienably his own. In *Lady Windermere's Fan* and *A Woman of No Importance* and *An Ideal Husband,* you are aware of the mechanism—aware of Sardou. In all of them there is, of course, plenty of humanity, and of intellectual force, as well as of wit and humour; and these qualities are the more apparent for the very reason that they are never fused with the dramatic scheme, which was a thing alien and ready-made. The Sardou manner is out-of-date; and so those three plays do, in a degree, date. It is certain that Oscar Wilde would later have found for serious comedy a form of his own, and would have written serious comedies as perdurable as his one great farce.

In *The Importance of Being Earnest* there is a perfect fusion of manner and form. It would be truer to say that the form is swallowed up in the manner. For you must note that not even in this play had Oscar Wilde invented a form of his own. On the contrary, the bare scenario is of the tritest fashion in the farce-writing of the period. Jack pretends to his niece, as an excuse for going to London, that he has a wicked brother whom he has to look after. Algernon, as an excuse for seeing the niece, impersonates the wicked brother. Jack, as he is going to marry and has no further need of a brother, arrives with the news of the brother's death; and so forth. Just this sort of thing had served as the staple for innumerable farces in the 'sixties and 'seventies and 'eighties—and would still be serving so if farce had not now been practically snuffed out by musical comedy. This very ordinary clod the magician picked up, turning it over in his hands—and presto! a dazzling prism for us.

How was the trick done? It is the tedious duty of the critic to ask such questions, and to mar what has been mere delight by trying to answer them. Part of the play's fun, doubtless, is in the unerring sense of beauty that informs the actual writing of it. The absurdity of the situation is made doubly absurd by the contrasted grace and dignity of everyone's utterance. The play abounds, too, in perfectly chiselled apothegms—witticisms unrelated to action or character, but so good in themselves as to have the quality of dramatic surprise. There are perhaps, in the course of the play, a dozen of those merely verbal inversions which Oscar Wilde invented, and which in his day the critics solemnly believed—or at any rate solemnly declared—to be his only claim to the title of wit. And of these inversions perhaps half-a-dozen have not much point. But, for the rest, the wit is of the finest order. 'What between the duties expected of one during one's lifetime, and the duties exacted after one's death, land has ceased to be either a profit or a pleasure. It gives one a position, and prevents one from keeping it up. That's all that can be said about land.' One cannot help wishing it were all that 'the Dukes' had had to say recently. It is a perfect presentation of the case which they have presented so lengthily and so maladroitly. And it is only a random sample of the wit that is scattered throughout *The Importance of Being Earnest.* But, of course, what keeps the play so amazingly fresh is not the inlaid wit, but the humour, the ever-fanciful and inventive humour, irradiating every scene. Out of a really funny situation Oscar Wilde would get dramatically the last drop of fun, and then would get as much fun again out of the correlative notions aroused in him by that situation. When he had to deal with a situation which, dealt with by any ordinary dramatist, would be merely diagrammatic, with no real fun at all in it, always his extraneous humour and power of fantastic improvisation came triumphantly to the rescue. Imagine the final scenes of this play treated by an ordinary dramatist! How tedious, what a signal for our departure from the theatre, would be the clearing-up of the mystery of Jack Worthing's parentage, of the baby in the handbag, the manuscript in the perambulator! But the humour of the writing saves the situation, makes it glorious. Lady Bracknell's recital of the facts to the trembling Miss Prism—'Through the elaborate investigations of the Metropolitan police, the perambulator was discovered at midnight, standing by itself in a remote corner of Bayswater. It contained the manuscript of a three-volume novel of more than usually revolting sentimentality'—and Miss Prism's subsequent recognition of the hand-bag by 'the injury it received through the upsetting of a Gower Street omnibus in younger and happier days' and by 'the stain on the lining caused by the explosion of a temperance beverage, an incident that occurred at Leamington'—these and a score of other extraneous touches keep us laughing whole-heartedly until the actual fall of the curtain.

—Max Beerbohm, "A Classic Farce,"
1909, *Last Theatres,* ed. Rupert
Hart-Davis, 1970, pp. 508–511

JOHN DRINKWATER (1923)

John Drinkwater was a novelist, poet, dramatist, and critic. This extract states that *The Importance of Being Earnest* was Wilde's greatest aesthetic triumph, a view Drinkwater delivers over a quarter of a century after the play's first production. Drinkwater's review of the play begins by making a considerable number of astute remarks about Wilde the man: that Wilde found it impossible to actually live as beautifully as he wished and as he suggested was possible in his art; that this situation was born from his own emotional inadequacy; and that such an incapacity gave rise to a sense of cynicism and sentimentality that was occasionally and detrimentally apparent in much of his art. Drinkwater believes that *The Importance of Being Earnest* is the one piece of Wilde's art that escapes these problems and that in its very portrayed insincerities one might

find a sincere aesthetic perspective on the world. Like many other critics
before him, Drinkwater suggests that this play escapes the moral order
of everyday life and finds a contrasting joy in life, what this extract admiringly states to be a comedy of pure fun.

It may sound wilful to say of a man who, more perhaps than any other of
his generation, attacked the bourgeoisie with great if rather fantastic courage
that his chief defect as an artist was want of taste. And yet, considering his
work as a whole, that seems to be the truth about Oscar Wilde. He cared
very much about art and said many brave and challenging things for it. He
was preoccupied always with it, and as an artist himself he tried honourably
to deal with an experience of life which, although it was turgid and forlorn,
was real enough. Mere reality of experience, however, is not enough. Before
he can create largely the artist must not only have his personal vitality of
experience, but he must love that experience passionately, however dark its
mood may be. In reading most of Wilde's poetry, all his plays but one, and
his critical studies, one feels, while all the time admiring a very rare executive
gift, that here is a man who, for the most part, instead of standing bravely
by his experience was trying to escape from it. This is not at all to suggest
that he was a man lacking in common courage; few men have met disaster
of fortune and temperament with so gallant a bearing. It is in a way easy for
the protagonist in one of the great tragic movements of nature to meet fate
fearlessly. But there is little enough of exaltation for the man who is destroyed
not by passion but a merely trivial wasting of his own character. But, while
Wilde did not lack courage of that kind, he was deficient in that other courage
which makes the artist loyal to himself at whatever cost. If the artist cannot
approach universal beauty surely through the channels of his own emotional
life, he is certain to fall into cynicism or sentimentality or both, and this is
what Wilde did in most of his work. He was sensitive enough to the profound
normal beauty of life, free play of character, charity, understanding, and the
mystery of sacrifice. But he saw it all afar off, pathetically, as something which
he cared for devotedly, but could not himself quite be out of the resources of
his own nature. And so passion is replaced by mere wistfulness, and the tragic
realisation at which he aimed is continually sentimentalised. And at moments
when the artist's awareness of this defect in himself left him with nothing but
a forlorn sense that the beauty of which he knew so well was never quite
truly his own, cynicism became his inevitable refuge. It is fair to say that
this with Wilde did not happen often. As in the conduct of his own unhappy

life, so in his art he did strive with courage towards what he knew to be the better reason. But the final issue remains that his work taken as a whole in its brilliance and pathos misses the profounder qualities of humour and passion, and it must be remembered that this was not by deliberate intention.

Once, however, Wilde's own nature, with all its limitations, worked clearly in delight of itself, and achieved what is in its own province a perfect work of art. *The Importance of Being Earnest* is not really a comedy of manners in the sense of being primarily a criticism of the follies into which a society is betrayed by its conventions, and a tearing off of the masks. Nor is it primarily a comedy of wit, sure and sustained as the wit is. Attempts have been made to derive the play in some measure from the Restoration masters, but without much conviction, and while the manner employed by Wilde has clearly influenced some later writers notably St. John Hankin, *The Importance of Being Earnest* really forms a class in English drama by itself. It is in mere simplicity that one says that it seems to be the only one of Wilde's works that really has its roots in passion. Every device of gaiety and even seeming nonsense is employed to keep the passion far back out of sight, and, if it were otherwise, the play would not be the masterpiece it is. But the passion is there. That is to say that the play is directly an expression of that part of Wilde's own experience which was least uncontaminated and in which he could take most delight. And this meant that all his great gifts as a craftsman were for once employed in work where, with insincerity almost as the theme, there was more sincerity than in anything else he did. Plays like *Salomé* and *The Florentine Tragedy* are at best little more than virtuosity, while *The Woman of No Importance, Lady Windermere's Fan* and *The Ideal Husband*, although they may have many of the qualities that mark Wilde's one great achievement, are on the whole frank surrenders to a fashion of the theatre which Wilde had too good a brain not to despise. But in *The Importance of Being Earnest* there is neither virtuosity nor concession. It is a superb and original piece of construction, with several moments of stage mastery which can hardly be excelled in comedy, and packed throughout with a perfect understanding of dramatic speech. One has only to recall any scene in the play and place it beside almost any of the successful comedies that one sees in the ordinary run of theatre production, to see how definitely apart that greatness is set which comes of having not three words in seven dramatically right but seven in seven. But when art comes to this excellence of form it can only mean excellence of life at the springs, and flowing through *The Importance of Being Earnest* is the surest and clearest part of Wilde's life. There was much, perhaps everything, in the more profoundly moving story of man that Wilde saw always imperfectly or not at all. But he did see, with a subtlety that can hardly be matched in our dramatic literature, that the common intrigues of daily life are not really the moralist's province at all, but interesting only for the sheer amusement that can be got out of them. Shakespeare gave to the English stage a comedy as full of poetic passion as great tragic art, Ben Jonson the comedy of humours, and Congreve and his fellows the true comedy of manners, but Wilde in his one masterpiece brought into the same company of excellence the comedy of pure fun.

> —John Drinkwater, vol. viii,
> *The Complete Works of Oscar Wilde,*
> New York, 1923, introduction, pp. ix–xiv,
> reprinted in *The Muse in Council,* 1925

DE PROFUNDIS

E.V. LUCAS (1905)

Edward Lucas was a travel writer, essayist, the director of Methuen and Company, and edited in 1919 a collection of Wilde's reviews, *A Critic in Pall Mall.* In this extract written for the *Times Literary Supplement*, Lucas reviews Wilde's *De Profundis*, the long letter composed by Wilde, while he was in prison, for Alfred Douglas, and published by Robert Ross after Wilde's death.

Lucas suggests, as others have done in earlier extracts cited in this volume, that Wilde's letter is not an instance of "souls laid bare" but rather a cleverly crafted "counterfeit" of emotion; it is a work of art, rather than a confession. Lucas suggests that Wilde's poses were impossible for the imprisoned artist to shed, that the lines of *De Profundis* do not display a "broken man" at all. Wilde simply could not consciously tell the truth. Lucas describes Wilde's genius as lying in his, and his art's, "lawless irresponsibility" or "humorous inconsistency." For Lucas, it is when Wilde took his poses seriously that his work and life suffered. He was always a wit but could descend from humor into pedantry (showing off one's learning). Students might compare the distinction between wit and humor made by Max Beerbohm in earlier extracts.

Lucas finds the value of Wilde's *De Profundis* in the capacity of the artist to overcome his trials. The idea of the individual overcoming life through art is, of course, precisely what Wilde had always proclaimed was the basis of his aesthetic philosophy.

This is an unfailingly and now and then poignantly interesting work; it contains some beautiful prose, some confessions that cannot leave the reader unmoved and may even touch him a little with shame at his own fortunate rectitude; and a passage of theological conjecture that is most engaging in its ingenuity and of a very delicate texture. The book contains all this and more, and yet while realizing the terrible conditions under which it was written, and possessed by every wish to understand the author and feel with him in the utter wreck of his career, it is impossible, except very occasionally, to look upon his testament as more than a literary feat. Not so, we find ourselves saying, are souls laid bare. This is not sorrow, but its dexterously constructed counterfeit.

Yet when we ask ourselves in what other way we would have had Oscar Wilde's cry from the depths we are unable to reply; for the bitter truth is that he was probably unable to cry from the depths at all; perhaps, paradoxical as it may sound, was unable really to be in the depths. For this book might be held to fortify the conviction that there is an armour of egotism which no arrow of fate can pierce. How Wilde felt in the watches of the night in that squalid cell we can only conjecture; this book gives little clue. In this book he is as much as ever the bland and plausible artist in phrase, except that for the most part he is advocating a new creed of humility in place of earlier gospels. Even in prison, even at the end of everything he most valued, his artifice was too much for him; his poses were too insistent—had become too much a part of the man—to be abandoned. If the heart of a broken man shows at all in this book, it must be looked for between the lines. It is not in them.

That a man who had travelled by Wilde's courses to Wilde's end should write, in prison, an analysis of his temperament, and a history of his ruin, coming therein to such conclusions as are here set forth, and during his task should pen no word that bore the mark of sincerity unadorned, is in its way a considerable feat. But it vitiates the book; or rather takes the book from the category of genuine emotion and places it among the *tours de force*. But it enables us now to know absolutely—what we had perhaps before guessed—that Oscar Wilde, however he may have begun life, grew to be incapable of deliberately telling the truth about himself or anything else. Being a man of genius, he often stumbled on it; but he could not say, "I will be truthful," and be truthful; he lost that power. We doubt if he was truthful even to himself towards the end. . . .

Wilde speaks in this little book of his artistic creed, his teaching, his philosophy of life; but it is very doubtful if he had ever really formulated one and made any sustained effort to understand it and conform to it. For his genius lay in lawlessness. He was essentially lawless, and his work is of value only when the author has forgotten that he is the exponent of a system. Every writer has somewhere an intimate personal gift which distinguishes him from every other writer—although it is often so minute as to escape detection. Wilde's particular and precise gift was lawless irresponsibility—humorous inconsistency is perhaps as good a description of it. If all his work could be spread out like an extinct river bed in the Klondike, a tiny thread of gold would be seen to break out here and there fitfully and freakishly within it. That vein of gold would represent those moments in Wilde's literary career when he forgot who he was and what he thought he stood for and allowed his native self to frolic and turn somersaults amid verities and conventions. Essentially an improviser and of hand-to-mouth intellect, he allowed himself to believe himself a constructive philosopher; essentially a mocker he was weak enough to affect to be a high priest of reverence. The result is that, although he essayed almost every variety of literary expression, in none except sheer irresponsibility did he come near perfection. We have always considered *The Importance of Being Earnest* his high-water mark of completed achievement; and we should associate with it those passages in his other writings where the same mood has play. Of Wilde's other work it is conceivable that industrious disciples might have produced it with more or less—perhaps sufficient—success. In any case it does not really matter. The failure of Wilde's life and the failure of his work have the same root; he could not resist temptation. We would not say that as a writer he was tempted in the same degree as a pleasure-loving man; his artistic conscience was made of better stuff than his civic conscience; but he was tempted often, and he always fell. His real destiny was to be an improviser, an inconsistent but often inspired commentator, a deviser of paradoxes, an exponent of the unfamiliar side of things; instead, he thought himself a leader of men, a prophet, a great writer of prose, a serious dramatic poet. By nature a witty and irresponsible Irishman, he grew to believe himself a responsible neo-Hellene. Born to be a lawless wit he was often something very like a pedant. Had he possessed a sense of humour he might have been saved— another illustration of the total independence of humour and wit. . . .

What, then, is the value of *De Profundis?* Its value is this—that it is an example of the triumph of the literary temperament over the most disadvantageous conditions; it is further documentary evidence as to one of the most artificial natures produced by the nineteenth century in England; and here and there it makes a sweet and reasonable contribution to the gospel of humanity.

—E.V. Lucas, *Times Literary Supplement,*
February 24, 1905, pp. 64–65

G. Lowes Dickinson (1905)

Goldsworthy Lowes Dickinson was a political activist, historian, and Cambridge professor. In his book *Heretics*, the critic G.K. Chesterton had suggested that Dickinson was overly enamored of the classical Greeks' paganism, an aesthetic appreciation that Dickinson may well have found in Wilde's thought. In this extract, Dickinson, himself a homosexual, examines Wilde's downfall through a reading of *De Profundis*.

Dickinson sees in *De Profundis* a righteous "repentance" without "regret" and in Wilde's treatment only the latest example of the English public's failure to appreciate the individuality of the artist and its refusal to understand the inherent challenge to convention such individuality represents. Seeing Wilde as a Christlike martyr, Dickinson suggests that only the artist can save society, but, in the role of savior, he must be crucified by the very society he will redeem. It is, for Dickinson, to Wilde's credit that, like Christ, he embraced his suffering (Wilde had refused to take the opportunity to escape to France before his conviction), and the inevitable tragedy that faced him as an artist in English society. The extract concludes with Dickinson's assertion that the true shame of Wilde's downfall was represented by the inhumanity of those who mocked him upon his sentencing (bringing to mind the jeering faced by Christ on his way to execution). There is an understanding of the necessity of Wilde's fall in this extract as existing within the context of society's hatreds, his own character as an aesthetic challenge to society, and the absolute need for the salvation of those who fail to appreciate just what the artist accomplishes for the world.

―――――――――――――――――――

To Heine it seemed an unintelligible caprice in Shakespeare to have been born an Englishman. But Shakespeare, after all, has in him much that is English, and much that the English can genuinely admire. It is otherwise with some of our men of genius—with William Blake, for example, with Shelley, and, later, with Oscar Wilde. Of them we could make nothing, except martyrs. Blake, it is true, we ignored, as a lunatic; but Shelley we excommunicated; and Oscar Wilde we slowly murdered in prison. Why? What does it mean? Who is wrong? Is it we or they? It is time we asked ourselves these questions, and tried to answer them candidly, without sentimentality and without illusion.

The trouble between these men and us is, that they are artists and we are not. By which I do not mean that they were members of what has now become a "respectable" profession, "in the ordinary sense of that extraordinary word." I mean that they had, by nature, a certain attitude towards life, one which, of all attitudes, it is hardest for us, who are English, to understand. I will not attempt to describe it; I will let the artist speak for himself.

> . . . By the inevitable law of self-perfection, the poet must sing, and the sculptor think in bronze, and the painter make the world a mirror for his moods, as surely and as certainly as the hawthorn must blossom in spring, and the corn turn to gold at harvest-time, and the moon in her ordered wanderings change from shield to sickle, and from sickle to shield.

The artist is the man who lives by impulse, as we like to believe that Nature does. He is an individualist, though he has perhaps never heard of individualism. He develops himself, though perhaps he does not believe in self-development. By instinct, rather than conviction, he neglects conventions, rules, and forecasts. Above all, he ignores morality. "Morality does not help me. I am a born antinomian. I am one of those who are made for exceptions, not for laws." "I see that there is nothing wrong in what one does." But then, on the other hand: "I see that there is something wrong in what one becomes." To become the right thing, that is, the thing his impulses drive him to be, that is the artist's aim, or rather his instinct. Whatever happens to him he will accept, so only he can grow by it. And, among other things, he will accept sin, even though he repent of it. The *De Profundis*, in essence, is a confession of repentance; but the repentance involves no regret.

> I don't regret for a single moment having lived for pleasure. I did it to the full, as one should do everything that one does. There was no pleasure I did not experience. I threw the pearl of my soul into a cup of wine. I went down the primrose path to the sound of flutes. I lived on honey-comb. But to have continued the same life would have been wrong, because it would have been limiting. I had to pass on. The other half of the garden had its secrets for me also.

Such an attitude, by its mere existence, is a challenge to every law and every convention of society. The artist may or may not break these laws and conventions; that depends upon the character of his impulses. But he is a standing menace to them; he will always break them if he wants to. And it is this that society cannot forgive. Is society right or wrong?

Society represents morality; from which it does not follow that it represents virtue. Morality means rule, calculation, subordination, self-suppression. Every impulse it arrests with the questions: Whither do you tend? What are your consequences? Are you safe? Shan't I be sorry afterwards? Won't society suffer by my act? And morality is right to ask these questions. The pity is, that it should answer them so badly. Its answer is embodied in the whole fabric of our laws and conventions. And this fabric we are not simply wrong in declining to set aside, on the plea of some sudden cry of somebody's inmost self. Yet the cry is none the less imperative, none the less legitimate. The tragedy lies in the conflict between the soul and the soul's dead products. But in this conflict all the right is not on either side. The artist sins, and society sins; but society is the stronger, and the artist is crushed. The artist sins, because impulses are not necessarily good, either in themselves or in what they lead to. He has to sin if he is to grow, and, in proportion as he is a great artist, he turns to account his sin and its punishment. Society sins, because it has no impulses but only rules; and its rules at best are mere makeshifts. Society is at once the cause and the effect of Philistinism; for "he is the Philistine who upholds and aids the heavy, cumbrous, blind, mechanical forces of society, and who does not recognise dynamic force when he meets it, either in a man or a movement."

Thus it is that both the artist and society are always right and always wrong. The artist is the deliverer, and the only possible deliverer. But mankind can only be redeemed by crucifying its redeemer; and there is a sense in which the redeemer deserves to be crucified.

It follows from this, that the artist's life must be a tragedy. But tragedy, in a world like this, is not necessarily to be regretted. So, at least, it is deliberately affirmed by this latest of our victims. This pagan, this lover of beauty and joy, this subtlest, finest, and not least profound intelligence of our age, is suddenly blasted from the blue, hurled into a pit of infamy, shut out from the colour and light he loved as few have loved them, condemned to the most lingering of deaths, and a death, as it proved, not only of body, but of mind. And what has he to say about it? Only that he would not choose to have missed it; that suffering has crowned his life; and that the fact of suffering is itself a proof of love.

> It seems to me that love of some kind is the only possible explanation of the extraordinary amount of suffering that there is in the world. I cannot conceive of any other explanation. I am convinced that there is no other, and that if the world has indeed, as I have said, been built of sorrow, it has been built by the hands of love, because in no other way could the soul of man, for whom the world was made, reach the full stature of its perfection. Pleasure for the beautiful body, but pain for the beautiful soul.

Never has the Christian religion been more triumphantly vindicated than by this pagan whom Christians have abhorred.

But, even though it be true that there are cases where suffering may redeem, that does not excuse those who inflict the suffering. On this point, too, let us endeavour to "clear our minds of cant." Let it be admitted that there are matters in which the conduct of Oscar Wilde was such as every society, even the most enlightened and humane, would legitimately and reasonably condemn. Every society has a duty to protect the immature. Every society has a duty, and one more extensive than any society has ever yet admitted, to control sexual relations in the interest of the children to be born of them. But everything beyond that is a question of private morals and taste. Now the private morals and taste of our society are not such that it has a right to throw the first stone at any man. And our law, on the matter in question, is a mere survival of barbarism, supported, not by reason, but by sheer prejudice. It rests on no knowledge, no principle, no common sense; it rests on our instinct to persecute what we cannot understand. Oscar Wilde may have sinned, not only, as he admits, against himself, but against society. But who shall measure the moral gulf by which he is removed from the crowd of fallen women and sensual men who mobbed him at the gates of the court, who jeered at him on the platform of the railway station, and pointed at this man of genius, no word of whose message they could comprehend, the index of their gross and prurient scorn? It is of such elements, among others, that the society that condemns the artist is composed. Is the account clear between him and them?

And there is another point. Let us ignore the iniquities of opinion and of the law. Let us suppose that Oscar Wilde was as great a criminal as he was judged to be by all the basest and some of the finer elements of our society. Even so, was it right or, let us say, was it wise, to treat him as we did? This is a question which touches our whole system of punishment, and affects the case, not only of this isolated man of genius, but of hundreds and thousands of dumb and obscure offenders.

—G. Lowes Dickinson, *Independent Review,*
April 1905, pp. 375–377

Hugh Walker "The Birth of a Soul: (Oscar Wilde: The Closing Phase)" (1905)

Hugh Walker was a professor of English and philosophy at St. David's College, Lampeter (now the University of Wales, Lampeter). He published several volumes of criticism of literature, a number dealing with the Victorian period.

In this extract, Walker examines *De Profundis* as a response to the question of whether there is a way in which an individual's transgression can be converted into a moral benefit. Wilde believed that the pursuit of pleasure was not wrong in and of itself but only if that was the sole pursuit of the individual. The student can compare this belief to the statements made about epicureanism by Walter Pater in his review, previously cited in this volume, and also as suggested by Wilde's novel, *The Picture of Dorian Gray*. It is the understanding that suffering brings redemption to the individual that Walker claims was Wilde's lesson in *De Profundis* and "The Ballad of Reading Gaol," stating that the reader can observe that even if the poem does not seem to reveal its author's appreciation for the suffering he had undergone within the prison system, the letter had already proclaimed that appreciation when it was written between the walls of a cell. Walker is sensitive, as others have been, to the possibility of *De Profundis* being a pose, but he sees in "Reading Gaol" a sincerity lacking in all of Wilde's earlier works.

Walker analyzes the manner in which Wilde renders the belief that sin and suffering are inextricably linked, and, in their relationship, "beautiful, holy things and modes of perfection." The extract suggests that the justification for the suffering undergone by Wilde, pain made possible and necessary only through his sin, was the change in temperament and perspective it brought to the writer's life. This is what Walker describes as "the birth of a soul," as if Wilde was "begotten by sin and born of agony." He believes that Wilde's "birth" was not only made possible by his punishment but also only *because* of his sin. Walker claims that this "dangerous" idea is explored more profoundly in "Reading Gaol" and *De Profundis* than had occurred in nineteen centuries of Christianity. Students can contrast Walker's views on Wilde's "rebirth" to the several other extracts in this volume querying Wilde's sincerity and his conversion from an epicurean philosophy.

Forty years ago Robert Browning declared that, besides "the incidents in the development of a soul," there was little that was worth study; and all his poetry proves that he not only said it with his lips but believed it in his heart. If he was right, how supereminent must be the interest of an incident, or a group of incidents, the effect of which is so great that it is best described, not as the development of a soul, but as its re-birth! Such is the supreme interest which belongs to the two books, *De Profundis* and *A Ballad of Reading Gaol,* written by Oscar Wilde after the awful overthrow of his disgrace, condemnation and imprisonment. Whoever compares these books with any of Wilde's earlier writings, whether in prose or in verse, must surely be driven to the conclusion that their author was the child of a second birth in a sense far deeper than that which is usually attached to the glibly-repeated phrases of traditional theology. He may even be led to question the propriety of speaking about the "ruin" of Wilde, though Wilde applies the word to himself. "I must," he says, "say to myself that I ruined myself, and that nobody great or small can be ruined except by his own hand." Yet the question suggested by the two books above named is whether the apparent ruin was not in reality salvation; and whether, in the eye of infinite wisdom, the whole process of sin, and degradation, and suffering, might not be just the process most to be desired for such a man as Wilde. His condemnation smirched Wilde for ever with the "bar sinister" of the prison, made his name a name of reproach, and himself an outcast from society; but it led to the production of two works which, in their moral depth and permanent significance, dwarf all he had before written, all that he gave promise of writing. The tree is known by its fruit. Could such a tree have borne such fruit unless it had been watered by the bloody sweat of those appalling sufferings? Would anything but the utter disgrace and infamy of the sentence have wrung from Wilde the indispensable bloody sweat? But if the sufferings were necessary, then the sins from which they sprang were necessary too; and in that case it would seem that we must modify the ordinary conception of the nature of sin and suffering. Carlyle in a noble figure reminds us that the rose is none the less a rose although it springs from a dungheap. The metaphor is flung at that realism which belittles the higher elements of humanity because they are inseparably associated with the animal part. We accept it as a fine expression of the truth; but we probably shrink from asking ourselves what may be the components of that heap from which the rose draws its life. Neither, fortunately, is there the least necessity of descending to details; but *De Profundis* irresistibly impels us to ask the question whether there is any form of evil which is absolutely, irredeemably and immutably evil. We are accustomed to think of certain forms of evil as being capable of transformation into good. The suffering which is brought upon us by the action of others, or that which is due to our own inadvertent transgression, may be matter for thanksgiving. The baser passions are, we know, no more identical with the family affections, which are the glory of humanity, than is the festering corruption at the roots identical with the beautiful flower. Both have undergone a transformation "into something rich and strange." But dare we apply this same conception to the sins which we are conscious of committing against our own higher nature, which we feel have degraded us? Is there any moral alchemy which can alter the character of lying, and slander, and covetousness, and the thousand forms of impurity? This is the question which *De Profundis* forces us to raise. Wilde was neither the first to ask it nor the first to answer it; but probably no one else has so vividly illustrated the answer by his own life and work.

We need not lift the curtain from Wilde's history farther than he has lifted it himself in *De Profundis*. There he tells us, sufficiently for the purpose, what he was before his life was cleft in twain by the closing of the prison doors behind him. "The gods had given me almost everything," he says. "But I let myself be lured into long spells of senseless and sensual ease. I amused myself with being a *flâneur*, a dandy, a man of fashion. I surrounded myself with the smaller and the meaner minds. I became the spendthrift of my own genius, and to waste an eternal youth gave me a curious joy. Tired of being on the heights, I deliberately went to the depth in the search for new sensation." . . . "It was always springtime once in my heart. My temperament was akin to joy. I filled my life to the very brim with pleasure, as one might fill a cup to the very brim with wine." Nor must it be supposed that Wilde ever, even doing his imprisonment, turned his back completely upon his old life, or wholly renounced the principles which governed it. The new conception which filled his mind in prison was that they were, not so much false, as partial and one-sided. "I don't," he says, "regret for a single moment having lived for pleasure. I did it to the full, as one should do everything that one does. There was no pleasure I did not experience. I threw the pearl of my soul into a cup of wine. I went down the primrose path to the sound of flutes. I lived on honeycomb. But to have continued the same life would have been wrong, because it would have been limiting. I had to pass on."

The mistake, then, in Wilde's opinion, was, not in living for pleasure, but in living for that *alone*. He had been unfaithful to his own resolution, "to eat of the fruit of all the trees in the garden of the world": he had confined himself to those which grew on "the sunlit side of the garden." Richly endowed with genius, and with that charm which does not always accompany genius, even in his youth the apostle of a school, master of epigram and paradox, "the glass of fashion," he could say with truth that the gods had given him almost everything; and his friends might well think that he had but to go on with the same almost god-like ease, in order to make his life one triumphal procession. Yet they were certainly wrong. Wilde stood in a false relation to life. The elegancies would have palled, the pleasures would have cloyed, one ray of nature's sun would have revealed the theatrical falsity of the light.

Artistically, even,—the one thing which Wilde cared for—he would have become intolerable. The phrase-monger speedily wears himself out, the man who is always in a pose ends by becoming ridiculous. When he spoke condescendingly of the Atlantic Ocean, Wilde revealed to the discerning the goal towards which he was travelling. He had to learn something which was yet concealed from him.

Wilde learnt the indispensable lesson not voluntarily, but by the sternest of necessities. He had been told the truth, but he refused to believe it. "My mother," he says, "who knew life as a whole, used often to quote to me Goethe's lines, written by Carlyle in a book he had given her years ago, and translated by him, I fancy, also:—

Who never ate his bread in sorrow,
    Who never spent the midnight hours
Weeping and waiting for the morrow,—
    He knows you not, ye heavenly powers."

Wilde "absolutely declined to accept or admit the enormous truth hidden" in these lines. He "could not understand it." That his eyes might be opened, he had to pass within the prison doors,—to stand at Clapham Junction, manacled, in a garb of shame, the loadstone of all eyes as if he were some cynosure of the nether pit,—to think the dreadful thoughts of "the man who had to swing," and to realise the horror of the doom with a vividness far beyond the reach of the criminal's own mind. What such experiences must have meant to a bundle of nerves like Wilde, even his own words can but very imperfectly tell: no one else can attempt to tell it at all. Not often have such experiences been narrated by the man to whom they have come; where, except in these books, are they to be found narrated by such a "lord of language" as Wilde? No words can exaggerate, few minds can comprehend, the intensity of the mental sufferings of such a man in such a position. *De Profundis* and the *Ballad of Reading Gaol* show, as perhaps no other books have ever shown, the immensity of the difference which may divide punishments nominally the same. They illustrate in a startling fashion the crudity of human justice. And yet perhaps their effect upon Wilde may be the best vindication of its methods. The stolid criminal would certainly not have suffered as Wilde did; but neither would he have found Wilde's redemption.

It is the revelation of the effect of such a discipline of sin and punishment and suffering that gives Wilde's last two books their unique value; and it is herein too that we find their deepest agreement. In more ways than one *De*

Profundis is widely different from the *Ballad of Reading Gaol.* The fact that the former is in prose and the latter in verse is not important; for in conception both are poetical and tragic. But the spirit is different, as the circumstances of composition were different. *De Profundis,* written in prison, is more submissive. It does indeed condemn the system of punishment: "The prison style is absolutely and entirely wrong." But Wilde adds that "the spirit of the Christ who is not in the churches, may make it, if not right, at least possible to be borne without too much bitterness of heart." *Reading Gaol,* written after the prisoner's release, indicates a reaction. The picture of the warders "strutting up and down," keeping "their herd of brutes," and of their mockery of "the swollen purple throat," is full charged with bitterness; and it is doubtful whether anyone would infer from the ballad that sense of obligation to the prison officials, or at least to the Governor, which Wilde expresses in the letter prefixed to *De Profundis.* The reader perceives that, notwithstanding his condemnation of the prison system, the author of the ballad was profoundly indebted to that system; but he does not perceive that the poet himself was conscious of the debt. The chief purpose of *De Profundis,* on the other hand, is to proclaim it. Society is wrong in its treatment of the offender, the prison system is wrong,—yet in spite of the wrong there comes to him, through the treatment and through the system, the boon of a deeper and a larger life.

In some ways, therefore, the *Ballad of Reading Gaol* seems to show that Wilde was reverting towards something less alien from his former self than were his thoughts in prison; and on that account it may be held to justify the suspicion that the change in his character was less complete and profound than it would be judged from *De Profundis* to be. In at least one respect, however, and that the most vital, the *Ballad* shows continued progress along the same line. It is the most sincere of all Wilde's writings. *De Profundis* is incomparably more sincere than any of his earlier works; but the greatest flaw in it is the suggestion conveyed by some passages that perhaps after all the writer is only posing. That this is so is no matter for wonder; it would be marvellous, rather, if even such a tremendous catastrophe as his had all at once revolutionised the inborn disposition or the acquired character of the man. Wilde had breathed the breath of artifice and affectation; and even the prison could not all at once sweep it away and replace it with an atmosphere of simple truth and sincerity. But in the ballad every line bears its own guarantee of sincerity. The thoughts which the author expresses or suggests may be wrong; but it is impossible to doubt that they are the thoughts of a man deeply in earnest. Here, then, *De Profundis* is inferior; yet not so inferior as to be tainted in its essence. As the *Ballad of Reading Gaol* carries a guarantee in its tone, so does *De Profundis* in its substance. The thoughts in it are beyond, immeasurably beyond, Wilde's former range; the reader is forced to believe in their sincerity, because he feels certain that they would never have occurred to such a man by the mere exercise of imagination. He had to die to society, and almost to himself, in order that he might live again with alien powers and with thoughts hitherto inconceivable by him. It is significant that he believed his central conception to have been expressed only once before, and even then to have been misunderstood; yet he must have read it in one of the great poets of his own day. He read it; but only the prison experience gave him the key to its meaning.

To expect in Wilde an ordinary reformation, even as the result of such an experience, would be to misunderstand the man; and he leaves us in no doubt about the futility of such an expectation. "I need not tell you," he says, "that to me reformations in morals are as meaningless and vulgar as Reformations in theology. But while to propose to be a better man is a piece of unscientific cant, to have become a deeper man is the privilege of those who have suffered. And such I think I have become." Such, indeed, he had become. The worshipper of beauty who had turned away from sorrow and suffering of all kinds as modes of imperfection, now declares that pain is the indispensable condition of the highest beauty of all. He who had said that there was "enough suffering in one narrow London lane to show that God did not love man," now writes: "It seems to me that love of some kind is the only possible explanation of the extraordinary amount of suffering that there is in the world. I cannot conceive of any other explanation. I am convinced that there is no other, and that if the world has indeed, as I have said, been built of sorrow, it has been built by the hands of love, because in no other way could the soul of man, for whom the world was made, reach the full stature of its perfection. Pleasure for the beautiful body, but pain for the beautiful soul."

Part of Wilde's doctrine is, as has been already said, commonly accepted; and he himself was, in the earlier part of his life, exceptional in denying it. Theologians would have no difficulty in accepting Wilde's words in the passage quoted above: they would consider them admirably orthodox. They have taught the moral value of suffering, and their recognition of it is the most vital difference between their ethical teaching and that of the Greek philosophers. It is likewise the most vital difference between the teaching of Christianity and that of Judaism: "prosperity," says Bacon, "is the blessing of the Old Testament; adversity is the blessing of the New." But while they have taught this, theologians have, at the same time, drawn the broadest of lines between suffering and sin. They conceive of the former as something which is, somehow, necessary for the moral good of humanity, though they cannot understand it. "Clergymen," says Wilde, "and people who use phrases without wisdom sometimes talk of suffering as a mystery. It is really a revelation." But while they regard suffering as, though mysterious, necessary, and in some uncomprehended way right, towards sin their attitude is altogether negative. It would be right to court suffering for a good cause; but many have taught that to commit the most venial sin, were it even to secure the most transcendent good, would be to deserve damnation. And probably many more, who are unable to banish all sense of proportion in face of the word "sin," would feel themselves holier men if they only could do so. To them sin is evil, absolute and immitigable. The ecclesiastical conception of saintship rests almost wholly on the conviction that it is a higher thing to have committed no sin than, in achieving great results, to have gathered also the spots and stains of a world where evil is plentifully mingled with good. The view is negative rather than positive; innocence is set above a life of strenuous but not immaculate virtue.

Now, it is important to notice that Wilde recognises no such absolute distinction between, on the one hand, a form of evil called sin, which is always and incurably evil, and which has to be simply blotted out by a special act of divine grace; and, on the other hand, forms of evil called pain and suffering, which are even essential to the highest good. Not only so, but he justifies his own view by a reference to the teaching of Christ. "The world had always loved the saint as being the nearest possible approach to the perfection of God. Christ, through some divine instinct in him, seems to have always loved the sinner as being the nearest possible approach to the perfection of man. His primary desire was not to reform people, any more than his primary desire was to relieve suffering. To turn an interesting thief into a tedious honest man was not his aim. In a manner not yet understood of the world, he regarded sin and suffering as being in themselves beautiful holy things and modes of perfection."

There is a suggestion of phrase-making in the sentence about the interesting thief and the tedious honest man. There can be no doubt that Christ did aim at turning the thief, although he might be interesting, into an honest man, even if in the process he became tedious; and Wilde must have been perfectly well aware of the fact. The sentence is one of the lingering traces of insincerity which mar the book. But the main thought expressed was deeply and seriously felt. Wilde had indeed come to regard "sin and suffering as being "beautiful holy things and modes of perfection"; and he believed that Christ so regarded them.

"It seems a very dangerous idea," he goes on. "It is—all great ideas are dangerous. That it was Christ's creed admits of no doubt. That it is the true creed I do not doubt myself.

"Of course the sinner must repent. But why? Simply because otherwise he would be unable to realise what he had done. The moment of repentance is the moment of initiation. More than that: it is the means by which one alters one's past. The Greeks thought that impossible. They often say in their Gnomic aphorisms, 'Even the Gods cannot alter the past.' Christ showed that the commonest sinner could do it, that it was the one thing he could do. Christ, had he been asked, would have said—I feel quite certain about it—that the moment the prodigal son fell on his knees and wept, he made his having wasted his substance on harlots, his swine-herding and hungering for the husks they ate, beautiful and holy moments in his life. It is difficult for most people to grasp the idea. I daresay one has to go to prison to understand it. If so, it may be worth while going to prison."

It should be noticed that there is in the former of these passages an apparent oversight of expression. Wilde speaks of Christ as having regarded "sin and suffering as being *in themselves* beautiful and holy things." When he comes to illustrate, what he says is that when the prodigal son fell on his knees and wept, he made his sins beautiful and holy moments in his life. The difference is important: the sins are no longer beautiful and holy *in themselves,* but in their results. The repentant prodigal is a better man—or, if Wilde prefers it, a deeper man—than many just men which need no repentance; but his sins alone, without the repenta would not make him better or deeper.

These paragraphs are the core of *De Profundis.* Out of the depths to which he had sunk, or from the heights towards which he was rising, Wilde proclaimed this startling gospel, that sin and suffering are beautiful holy things and modes of perfection. That is what one of the most appalling of all imaginable experiences had taught him. He appears to have believed that this doctrine was original with him, or rather that it was original with Christ, and that he was the first who had taken it from the teaching of Christ. He was not altogether right: it was not absolutely necessary—for all men, though probably it was for him—to go to prison in order to learn it. The doctrine is closely akin to that of Hegel, who likewise taught that good is evolved out of evil; and though Wilde, who tells us that metaphysics interested him very little and morality not at all, may well have neglected the philosopher, it is more strange that he had not detected the same teaching in the verse of Browning. One of the most frequently recurrent thoughts in Browning's poetry is that of the necessity of evil to progress. It runs through his work from beginning to end, appearing at least as early as *Sordello,* and finding perhaps its clearest and fullest expression in the last volume he ever published. It is the whole meaning of the poem *Rephan,* where the sentence pronounced upon the aspiring soul is, "Thou art past Rephan, thy place be Earth." And Browning as well as Wilde refuses to take shelter behind the distinction between suffering and sin. Both are necessary. The soul must be "by hate taught love." The Earth to which the growing spirit is sent is earth with all her innumerable forms of evil:—

Diseased in the body, sick in soul,
Pinched poverty, satiate wealth,—your whole
Array of despairs.

Doubtless Wilde read Browning at a time when such teaching was wholly alien from his mind, and for that reason missed the poet's meaning. He is less original than he believed himself to be; but he is even more interesting than he knew. For in one respect he is unique. He not only taught this doctrine, but he affords in his own person the most striking illustration of it. To him it came, not from books, but fresh stamped with the impress of truth from the mint of experience. From him it passes to the reader, not a mere theory, but a life. There, on the one hand, is Oscar Wilde, *flâneur* and dandy, treading the primrose path to the sound of flutes, sporting upon the surface of life, beautiful as a floating bubble played upon by the sunlight, and almost as evanescent,—here, on the other, is a new Oscar Wilde, branded with infamy, worn with suffering, but forced by that very infamy and suffering to work down towards the depths, where he finds and makes his own, as no one else had ever done, the thought of the greatest European philosopher and the most philosophic English poet of the nineteenth century. By that achievement he has probably made his fame permanent; and he has certainly made it impossible for any contemporary to ignore him.

A catastrophe more utter and apparently irretrievable than Wilde's can hardly be conceived. His very fame made it the more hopeless. Other prisoners might retire into obscurity, they could easily hide themselves from the few who knew them. But for him the whole earth was "shrivelled to a handsbreadth," and he must wear the brand of infamy in the face of day. It was just from the completeness of the ruin, in the worldly sense, that the new soul took its birth. With penetrating insight Wilde perceived that he must not attempt to deny his imprisonment, or to pretend that such an incident had never occurred in his life. Not only would the pretence in his case have been hopeless, but it would have been a blunder even if he could have succeeded in deceiving men. "I want," he says, "to get to the point when I shall be able to say quite simply, and without affectation, that the two great turning-points in my life were when my father sent me to Oxford, and when society sent me to prison." "To deny one's own experiences is to put a lie into the lips of one's own life. It is no less than a denial of the soul."

It is pathetic to observe this pleasure-loving spirit bent by an iron necessity to a fate as hard as the worst which mediaeval asceticism ever contrived for itself. But the justification of the suffering comes from the extraordinary change which it produced. "Most people," says he, "are other people. Their thoughts are someone else's opinions, their lives a mimicry, their passions a quotation." It is profoundly true; and, though to the end he did not suspect the fact, it is true of Wilde himself till the period of his imprisonment. He was, indeed, the leader of a fashion; but the fashion itself was an unconscious plagiarism from a highly artificial society. Until his terrible disaster Wilde had never been forced to dive into the depths of his own spirit; he had delighted to play on the surface. By compulsion he learnt wisdom.

The change worked in Wilde is so enormous that it may fairly be described as the birth of a soul. The new soul was begotten by sin and born of agony. Its life was short; and there is sad reason to fear that even before the close Wilde had slid far back towards the gulf from which he had emerged. Probably he had by his early career too completely sapped and undermined his own character to be capable of standing firm upon the height which he had gained. Yet even so the change was sufficient reward for the throes of birth; it was worth while to have trodden even such a wine-press of the wrath of God. The prodigal had fallen on his knees and wept, his soul had had one glimpse of the immortal sea, he had stood for a moment upon the peak in Darien; and however long had been his life, however stained with errors, weaknesses and vices, it must have been influenced by that transmuting experience. It had changed Wilde's whole view of life; and though he might have sinned deeply against himself, he could never have forgotten the "revelation" of suffering.

The most momentous question suggested by the amazing result is: Could the reformation have been brought about at a cheaper price? Could the new soul have been born of any other parentage? Would anything but that terrible suffering have given the apostle of aestheticism the depth and the earnestness necessary to conceive the *Ballad of Reading Gaol* and *De Profundis?* If not, for him it may have been worth while, not only to go to prison, but even to sin as deeply as he did. The idea may be, as he says, a dangerous one; but what if it be true? Have all the churches, in nineteen centuries, thrown such light upon the problem of evil as is shed by these two books in contrast with their author's earlier writings?

> —Hugh Walker, "The Birth of a Soul:
> (Oscar Wilde: The Closing Phase),"
> *Hibbert Journal,* January 1905, pp. 756–768

Chronology

〜〜〜　〜〜〜　〜〜〜

1854 Born in Dublin on October 16.

1871–74 Student at Trinity College, Dublin.

1874–78 Student at Magdalen College, Oxford, where in 1878 he won the Newdigate Prize for poetry and took a first-class degree in classics and humane letters.

1884 Married to Constance Lloyd on May 29.

1887–89 Serves as editor of *The Woman's World*.

1891 First meeting with his future lover, Lord Alfred Douglas, a rapacious poet. Publication of *The Picture of Dorian Gray, Intentions, Lord Arthur Savile's Crime* and *A House of Pomegranates*.

1892 *Lady Windermere's Fan:* first performance on February 20.

1893 *Salomé* published. *A Woman of No Importance* performed.

1895 *An Ideal Husband* first performed on January 3, and *The Importance of Being Earnest* first performed on February 14. Wilde sued the Marquess of Queensberry, Lord Alfred Douglas's father, for libel. The trial, lasting from April 3 to 5, resulted in the marquess's acquittal. This was followed by two trials in which Wilde faced criminal charges of homosexuality. The first, April 26 to May 1, ended in a hung jury, but the second, May 20 to 25, resulted in Wilde's conviction and subsequent imprisonment for two years of hard labor.

1897 Writes *De Profundis* in Reading Gaol as a letter to Lord Alfred Douglas. Departs for France on May 19, after his release from prison.

1898 "The Ballad of Reading Gaol" is published.

1900 Dies in Paris on November 30 at the age of forty-six.

Index

Characters in literary works are indexed by first name (if any), followed by the name of the work in parentheses